SELECTIVE PROSECUTION OF RELIGIOUSLY MOTIVATED OFFENDERS IN AMERICA

Scrutinizing The Myth of Neutrality

Joel Fetzer

Studies in American Religion
Volume 42

The Edwin Mellen Press
Lewiston/Queenston/Lampeter

Library of Congress Cataloging-in-Publication Data

Fetzer, Joel.
  Selective prosecution of religiously motivated offenders in
America : scrutinizing the myth of neutrality / by Joel Fetzer.
    p. cm. -- (Studies in American religion : vol. 42)
  Bibliography: p.
  Includes index.
  ISBN 0-88946-648-3
  1. Freedom of religion--United States. 2. Prosecution--United
States--Decision making. I. Title. II. Series: Studies in
American religion ; v. 42
  KF4783.F47   1989
  342.73' 0852--dc20
  [347.302852]   89-34122

> This is volume 42 in the continuing series
> Studies in American Religion
> Volume 42 ISBN 0-88946-648-3
> SAR Series ISBN 0-88946-992-X

A CIP catalog record for this book
is available from the British Library.

        The Edwin Mellen Press   The Edwin Mellen Press
             Box 450   Box 67
          Lewiston, NY   Queenston, Ontario
          USA 14092   CANADA L0S 1L0

                   The Edwin Mellen Press, Ltd.
                     Lampeter, Dyfed, Wales,
                  UNITED KINGDOM SA48 7DY

              Printed in the United States of America

**Dedicated in Memory of
Susan Ann Bernier
(1967-1988)**

Que son âme trouve le bonheur.

Contents

Tables and Chart

Acknowledgements

Much of the inspiration for this book came from intensive discussions with Professor Jeremy Rabkin of Cornell University's Department of Government. Professors Werner Dannhauser, Steven Jackson, E. W. Kelley, and Ronald King also deserve thanks for advice on matters in their respective areas of expertise.

The excellent reference staffs of the Library of Congress and Olin and Myron Taylor libraries helped me immensely with my research and in obtaining books through Inter-library Loan. For statistical data I must thank the National Abortion Federation, U.S. Immigration and Naturalization Service, the Statistical Reports Division of the Administrative Office of the U.S. Courts, and the many clerks of U.S. District Courts from whom I obtained docket sheets and sentencing orders.

Much of my research came from telephone conversations with knowledgeable individuals throughout the country. The insight of Michael McConnell (Chicago Religious Task Force on Central America), John Biermans (Unification Church of America), and Frank Madsen (Office of Senator Orrin Hatch) proved invaluable. Although they would not consent to being quoted by name, several individuals, both in and out of the government, aided me immeasurably by explaining the activities of their agencies or organizations.

The staff of the Edwin Mellen Press has been most helpful in transforming this work into a publishable and readable form.

Finally, I am indebted to my family and friends for advising me on various aspects of this project and for putting up with extended periods of maniacal behavior. I especially want to thank my parents, Carl and Joan Fetzer, and sister, Christy, for suggestions, funding, and sympathy; my *copains* in the *Maison française,* Scott Gunther and Yvon Guy, for overlooking my unorthodox sleeping habits; Gina Graziosi, for help with graphics in EXCEL; and Ansar Fayyazuddin for critiquing my tentative hypotheses.

Béni soit le nom de Yahvé.

Chapter I

Background and Statement of Hypotheses

According to official decisions by the Supreme Court, public policy and religion should not mix. The Court claims, for example, to be committed to the principle of "separation of church and state." In *Everson v. Board of Education* it ruled that the religion clause of the First Amendment ("Congress shall make no law respecting an establishment of religion or prohibiting the free exercise thereof")[1] "was intended to erect a 'wall of separation between church and State.'"[2] This metaphor seems to require governmental neutrality towards religion; in other words, religion should be kept out of legal and policy decisions as much as possible. Indeed, the Court in *Everson* came to a similar conclusion:

> The "establishment of religion" clause of the First Amendment means at least this: Neither a state nor the Federal Government can set up a church. Neither can pass laws which aid one religion, aid all religions, or prefer one religion over another. Neither can force nor influence a person to go to or to remain away from church against his will or force him to profess a belief or disbelief in any religion. *No person can be punished for entertaining or professing religious beliefs or disbeliefs,* for church attendance or non-attendance. . . . [The First Amendment] *requires the*

state to be a neutral in its relations with groups of religious believers and non-believers; it does not require the state to be their adversary. *State power is no more to be used so as to handicap religions than it is to favor them.*[3] [Emphasis added.]

The government, then, is not to take sides among religions, nor is it to treat its citizens differently based on their religious beliefs.

Despite the Supreme Court's official claim that the government should be neutral toward religion, it seems that in practice the government is sometimes less than blind to religious beliefs and motivations. Probably because it must explain its decisions to the public, the Supreme Court only rarely admits to making exceptions for religiously motivated offenders.[4] When in cases such as *Wisconsin v. Yoder*[5] it does, however, the Court tries its best to pretend it is not practicing favoritism towards religion, and often obscures this bias towards religion by explaining its actions without referring to religion, or by covering up its consideration of religion in official declarations of neutrality. Studying the official decisions of the Supreme Court to determine how the government considers religion, therefore, would not prove fruitful. Such decisions would only proclaim how the government should behave in theory. We must look elsewhere to discover how the federal government deals with religion in day-to-day politics.

Since religion is not supposed to play a part in their considerations, if government officials will have to explain their behavior to Congress or the public, they would seem less likely to take actions for which they could later be accused of improper religious considerations. One should find more religious considerations, then, where officials do not have to explain their actions. Since the number of decisions increases as the freedom to make those decisions increases, one would also expect to find more religious considerations in discretionary actions than in non-discretionary ones. The ideal place to study religious considerations in the government, then, would be where decision making is secret and highly discretionary.

On the federal level, that action which may best fulfill these two criteria for finding religious considerations may be the Department of Justice's decision to prosecute; for the decision to prosecute is informal, highly discretionary, usually secret, and rarely subject to outside review. Federal prosecutors do not have to explain their actions in front of congressional panels. Nor do Justice Department rules allow the release of internal memoranda to the public. Even senators are sometimes refused authorization to keep copies of prosecutorial documents they review at the Department.[6]

Federal attorneys do not hide the amount of discretion that they wield. The DOJ's official guidelines, *Principles of Federal Prosecution,* for example, openly describe the nature of their powers:

Under the federal criminal justice system, the prosecutor has wide latitude in determining when, whom, how, and *even whether to prosecute* for apparent violations of federal criminal law. The prosecutor's broad discretion in such areas as initiating or foregoing prosecutions, selecting or recommending specific charges, and terminating prosecutions by accepting guilty pleas has been recognized on numerous occasions by the courts. . . . This discretion exists by virtue of his status as a member of the Executive Branch, which is charged under the Constitution with ensuring that the laws of the United States be "faithfully executed."[7] [Emphasis added.]

Thus, the Department's prosecutors seem to view their discretionary powers as an integral part of their constitutional mandate to enforce the law.

Since "federal law enforcement resources and federal judicial resources are not sufficient to permit prosecution of every alleged offense over which federal jurisdiction exists,"[8] the Department must select defendants based on several factors, including "federal law enforcement priorities," the "nature and seriousness of the offense," and the "deterrent effect of prosecution."[9] In using this prosecutorial discretion, however, federal attorneys are not supposed to let the religion of a potential defendant enter into their decision:

> 6.   In determining whether to commence or recommend prosecution or take action, the attorney for the government should not be influenced by:
>   (a) the person's race; *religion;* sex; national origin; or political association, activities, or beliefs;[10] [Emphasis added.]

Thus, although according to official policy statements and traditional "American" principles of justice, the U.S. government should not take religion into account in deciding whom, how, and whether to prosecute, the evidence that I have collected seems to indicate that a potential defendant's religion occasionally *does* matter. In the three prominent criminal prosecutions that I have chosen to study, the defendants' religion appears to have played a major role in how the Executive Department's investigative and law enforcement mechanism responded to their alleged violations of the law. The case of the "Sanctuary Movement" appears to suggest that the government had strong reservations about prosecuting clergy and devout laypersons, and about arresting alleged felons and illegal aliens in a church building. In deciding whether to investigate and prosecute the Rev. Sun Myung Moon for tax evasion, the Internal Revenue Service and the Justice Department seem to have at least considered his status as the founder and leader of an international "cult." In the third case, the firebombing of abortion clinics by opponents of *Roe v. Wade,* the defendants' religious motivations seem to have played more than a secondary role in the government's treatment of them. In each of these three cases, then, it seems that the appropriate governmental agencies (the Department of Justice, Immigration and Naturalization Service, Internal Revenue Service, and Bureau of Alcohol, Tobacco and Firearms) have indeed let religious considerations influence their decisions to investigate and prosecute. The concluding chapter will deal with whether or not the government *should* take religion into account. The following case studies, however, will first try to establish what *does* occur in the decision to prosecute before proceeding to any normative questions.

These three cases seem to confirm a general hypothesis about governmental actions against religious groups: American society seems less likely to tolerate religion when one or both of the following conditions exist: 1. society regards a religion's belief system or its purely religious practices as extreme or dangerously outside the mainstream of contemporary religious belief and practices; and/or 2. society believes that the secular actions that a religion inspires are extreme or dangerously outside the society's limits of "normal" behavior. When either or both of these conditions occur, Americans will support action to "punish" the offenders. When these "offenses" take place on a national scale, the federal criminal justice system may be the most effective tool for enforcing these two societal norms.

Table I-1
The Relationship Between Americans' View of Offenders' Behavior and the Government's Treatment of Them

	Americans believe group's religious beliefs and practices are:	Americans believe group's religiously inspired actions are:	Federal government's treatment of group:
Sanctuary Movement	moderate	moderate	lenient
Reverend Moon	extreme	moderate	severe
Abortion-Clinic Bombers	moderate	extreme	severe

In order to illustrate this phenomenon, I have studied how three federal investigative agencies (the INS, IRS, and BATF) and the federal prosecutorial agency (the DOJ) have handled three representative cases. The prosecution of Rev. Moon for tax evasion shows how the federal government treats violators of the first norm (extreme religious practices or beliefs), and the case of the abortion-clinic bombers illustrates the government's reaction to violators of the second norm (extreme religiously inspired secular actions). As a "control" case, I consider the Sanctuary Movement, which our society seems to think is moderate both in the religious beliefs and practices of its participants, and in the religiously inspired actions they have taken.

The evidence I have collected suggests that Table I-1 is reasonable, and a simplified version of the causal model would appear as in Table I-2. In other words, the federal government takes note of whether most people approve or disapprove of a given religious group's behavior (i.e., whether or not most people consider the group to have followed the two hypothesized "norms"). The amount of public approval or disapproval helps determine whether government officials will investigate and prosecute, or whether they will leave a particular religious group alone.

Table I-2
Causal Model for the Government's Prosecutorial Response to Americans' Disapproval or Approval of Offenders' Behavior

American Society	---> *disapproves*	Federal Government	---> *prosecution or severity*	"offenders" punished
American Society	---> *approves*	Federal Government	---> *no prosecution or leniency*	"offenders" rewarded

Table I-3
The Government's Prosecutorial Behavior as a Function of Net Public Support Versus Net Public Opposition

		PUBLIC OPPOSITION:	
		High	*Low*
PUBLIC SUPPORT:	*High*	placate both sides	lenient treatment
	Low	severe treatment	no prosecution

A more sophisticated way to look at how the government perceives and acts upon the public's views of religiously motivated offenders would be to consider the support and opposition each offender or group of offenders has among various respectable constituencies. "Public approval" would mean more support from respectable ccnstituencies than opposition, and "public disapproval" would mean more opposition than support. A potential defendant's fortunes, then, would rise or fall depending on the degree of support and opposition from the constituencies. Illustrated graphically, cases of religiously motivated defendants should exhibit the pattern shown in Table I-3. Thus, if a group of offenders enjoys high support but low opposition, the government would try to avoid prosecuting or otherwise antagonizing them. If, however, opposition is high and support is low, the government would seem more likely to prosecute or otherwise act harshly against a group of potential defendants. In the more ambiguous case of both high support and high opposition, the federal government would try its best to placate both sides and antagonize neither, which obviously makes for contradictory policy and actions. When a group has both low support and low opposition, the government would probably not consider it a high enough priority to prosecute, and thus the group would benefit from apparently "lenient" treatment. According to the above hypothesis, the government would treat the three main groups I have studied and two similar cases as in Table I-4.

Of the cases studied, the Sanctuary Movement seems best to fit the category of high support/low opposition, and their treatment by the government seems to confirm my hypothesis. For the Movement enjoys strong support from almost all persuasions of the American religious community as well as from a broad base in Congress and the general populace. Its opposition, on the other hand, seems limited to a small section of right-wing activists and parts of the Reagan Administration. Probably as a consequence of this net support, the federal government has been very lenient with sanctuary workers who have violated U.S. immigration laws. Compared to similar secular offenders, they have been prosecuted and perhaps even investigated much less severely.

Table I-4
Case Studies Illustrating the Government's Prosecutorial Behavior as a Function of Net Public Support Versus Net Public Opposition

PUBLIC OPPOSITION:

		High	*Low*
PUBLIC SUPPORT:	*High*	televangelists/ Bakker's PTL Ministries (placate both sides)	Sanctuary Movement (lenient treatment)
	Low	Reverend Moon, abortion-clinic bombers (severe treatment)	"hustlers"/ "Reverend Ike" (no prosecution)

In the low support/high opposition category, however, the government has investigated and prosecuted almost mercilessly. As the leader of an international "cult," the Reverend Sun Myung Moon is, or at least was at the time of his trial for tax evasion, nearly universally despised. Although many religious leaders came to his defense when his case was on appeal to the Supreme Court, this eleventh-hour support appears to have been ineffective both because it came too late and because these clergy most likely lacked the backing of the laity which they supposedly represented. The IRS and DOJ, therefore, investigated and prosecuted Moon harshly.

Lacking any real support from even the "Pro-Life" community and vehemently condemned by "Pro-Choice" activists and the public at large, the abortion-clinic bombers also suffered harsher treatment at the government's hands as compared with similar, secularly motivated offenders.

"Televangelists" such as Jim Bakker appear to fit the high support/high opposition category. In Bakker's case, the government seems to have moved slowly and cautiously,[11] neither wanting to antagonize his many faithful supporters, nor wishing to appear "soft" on corruption among the clergy. When the scandal broke, the public and certain members of Congress did not hesitate to lambaste his "PTL Ministries,"[12] yet the government might not think it prudent to prosecute Bakker as much as it might like to because parts of the religious community and many of his former contributors still support him,[13] and many are criticizing governmental intrusion into what they believe is an internal, religious problem.[14]

An example of low support and low opposition, religious "hustlers" such as "Reverend Ike"[15] live extravagantly by more or less selling such religious articles as "blessed prayer clothes," while still benefitting from a religious tax exemption. In 1972, for example, Ike's virtual sale of what one writer has called "modern-day indulgences" brought him $6.5 million dollars in tax-exempt income,[16] and he claims that these contributions have made him so rich that he could drive a different Rolls Royce every day and "still have some left over."[17] Yet few people seem to care one way or the other about such an apparent charlatan, and according to my research, Reverend Ike has yet to face a federal investigation or prosecution for fraud or abuse of his religious tax exemption.

Notes

1.   U.S. Constitution, 1st Amendment.

2.   *Everson v. Board of Education*, 330 U.S. 1, 15-16 (1947).

3.   Ibid., pp. 15-16 & 18.

4.   See, for example, *Wisconsin v. Yoder*, 406 U.S. 205 (1972); *Berman v. United States*, 156 F.2d 377 (9th Cir.), *cert. denied*, 329 U.S. 795 (1946); and *United States v. Seeger*, 380 U.S. 163 (1965).

5.   *Wisconsin v. Yoder*, 406 U.S. 205 (1972).

6.   Senator Orrin G. Hatch, letter of January 5, 1988, to author.

7.   U.S. Department of Justice, *Principles of Federal Prosecution* (Washington, D.C.:   Government Printing Office, 1980), p. 1.   The following cases are cited as supporting the author's claims: *Oyler v. Boles*, 368 U.S. 448 (1962); *Newman v. United States*, 382 F.2d 479 (D.C. Cir. 1967); and *Powell v. Katzenbach*, 359 F.2d 234 (D.C. Cir. 1965), *cert. denied*, 384 U.S. 906 (1966).

8.   U.S. Department of Justice, p. 8.

9.   Ibid., p. 7.

10.   Ibid., p. 14.

11.   See, for example, "Grand Jury Opens Inquiry on PTL Ministries' Finances," *New York Times*, August 18, 1987, p. A17; William E. Schmidt, "Justice Dept. Sifting Bakker Finances," *New York Times*, May 29, 1987, p. A16; "3 Federal Agencies Open Criminal Inquiries on PTL Ministry," *New York Times*, June 11, 1987, p. A18; Gary Klott, "Tax Watch: The Key Issues In PTL Case," *New*

York Times, June 16, 1987; and "PTL Hearings," *New York Times,* June 24, 1987, p. A24.

12. "PTL Hearings," op. cit., p. A24; and William E. Schmidt, "TV Ministry Scandal Lampooned in South," *New York Times,* May 2, 1987, p. A1.

13. Phillip E. Hammond, "For Many, PTL Stands for Truth, Beauty, Not Scandal," *Los Angeles Times* June 4, 1987, part II, p. 5; and William E. Schmidt, "For Jim and Tammy Bakker, Excess Wiped Out a Rapid Climb to Success," *New York Times,* May 16, 1987, p. 8.

14. Michael Isikoff, "Evangelists Defend Funding Tactics, Decry House Hearings as Dangerous Precedent," *Washington Post,* October 7, 1987, p. C1.

15. The "Reverend Ike's" real name is Frederick Joseph Eikerenkoetter according to Clayton Riley, "The Golden Gospel of Reverend Ike," *New York Times,* March 9, 1975, p. 12.

16. Ibid., p. 12.

17. Clarence Waldron, "Rev. Ike Talks About Faith Healing in His Ministry," *Jet,* Vol. 69, December 2, 1985, pp. 30-32.

Chapter II

The Sanctuary Movement

The first case to be studied, the Sanctuary Movement, illustrates how the government treats religiously motivated offenders whose religion and actions are both moderate. The Movement's members come from practically all established religious groups, and no one objects to their strictly religious beliefs or practices. Nor does the Movement suffer from much criticism of its activities on behalf of Central Americans in this country. On the contrary, the Sanctuary Movement's many influential and vocal friends far outweigh its few enemies.

Probably as a result, both the Immigration and Naturalization Service and the Department of Justice have treated the sanctuary workers' law breaking with leniency. Only a handful of the Movement's tens of thousands of members have ever been arrested, and only two have spent any time in jail. Ever since Sanctuary's inception, the government has been extremely reluctant even to arrest these clergy and laypersons even though they blatantly flout U.S. immigration law and do not hesitate to embarrass the government and to criticize its immigration and foreign policy publicly.

* * * * * *

According to U.S. law, not only are aliens forbidden to enter this country without permission from the federal government, but U.S. citizens are usually forbidden to help those aliens who have already entered illegally. Citizens must not, for example, knowingly transport or shelter illegal aliens:

> Any person, including the owner, operator, pilot, master, commanding officer, agent, or consignee of any means of transportation who—
>
> 1) brings into or lands in the United States, by any means of transportation or otherwise, or attempts, by himself or through another, to bring into or land in the United States, by any means of transportation or otherwise;
>
> 2) knowing that he is in the United States in violation of law, and knowing or having reasonable grounds to believe that his last entry into the United States occurred less than three years prior thereto, transports, or moves, or attempts to transport or move, within the United States by means of transportation or otherwise, in furtherance of such violation of law;
>
> 3) willfully or knowingly conceals, harbors, or shields from detection, or attempts to conceal, harbor, or shield from detection, in any place, including any building or any means of transportation; or
>
> 4) willfully or knowingly encourages or induces, or attempts to encourage or induce, either directly or indirectly, the entry into the United States of—
>
> any alien, including an alien crewman, not duly admitted by an immigration officer or not lawfully entitled to enter or reside within the United States under the terms of this chapter or any other law relating to the immigration or expulsion of aliens,

shall be found guilty of a felony, and upon conviction thereof shall be punished by a fine not exceeding $2,000 or by imprisonment for a term not exceeding five years, or both, for each alien in respect to whom any violation of this subsection occurs: Provided, however, that for the purposes of this section, employment (including the usual and normal practices incident to employment) shall not be deemed to constitute harboring. [8 U.S.C. § 1324(a).]

The drafters of this legislation apparently considered its violation so harmful to the national interest that they made violators subject to felony charges and punishments of up to five years in prison *per alien*. Someone caught smuggling ten aliens, then, could spend as many as 50 years in jail and pay a fine of up to $20,000. And in general the law is seriously enforced. In the period from June 30, 1984, to June 30, 1986, for example, 315 felons were imprisoned, with a median sentence of 24 months,[1] for violations of 8 U.S.C. § 1324.

One would also expect that all violators would be prosecuted equally. In theory, the Department of Justice should not prosecute a higher percentage of one group of violators as opposed to any other. Yet even though members of the "Sanctuary Movement" boldly violate this statute, comparatively few have ever been convicted or even indicted for these violations. Although sanctuary workers openly flout U.S. immigration law and seem to invite the government to prosecute them, the DOJ seems reluctant to touch them. As will be shown later in more detail, the Sanctuary Movement's religious affiliations and its vocal supporters appear to have intimidated the DOJ into treating sanctuary workers more leniently than non-religious offenders.

Participants in the Sanctuary Movement do not pretend that they are obeying the law. In his "how-to guide" for the Movement, *Sanctuary: A Resource Guide for Understanding and Participating in the Central American Refugees' Struggle,* activist Gary MacEoin admits that Jim Corbett, co-founder of the Movement, and others actually smuggled "undocumented refugees" across the border between the U.S. and Mexico.[2] Corbett later justified his actions in the following terms:

> Because the U.S. government takes the position that aiding undocumented Salvadoran and Guatemalan refugees in this country is a felony, we have no middle ground between collaborating and resistance. . . . We can take our stand with the oppressed, or we can take our stand with organized oppression. We can serve the Kingdom, or we can serve the kingdoms of this world—but we cannot do both. . . . When the government itself sponsors the crucifixion of entire peoples and then makes it a felony to shelter those seeking refuge, *law-abiding protest merely trains us to live with atrocity.*[3] [Emphasis added.]

Corbett, then, did not hide the illegality of his smuggling and harboring operations.

The Sanctuary Movement's other co-founder, Reverend John M. Fife of Tucson, Arizona's Southside Presbyterian Church, even went so far as to write Attorney General William French Smith on March 23, 1982, telling him he was about to break the law by harboring Central Americans the INS would label "illegal aliens":[4]

> We take this action because we believe the current policy and practice of the U.S. government with

regard to Central American refugees is illegal and immoral. We believe our government is in violation of the 1980 Refugee Act and international law by continuing to arrest, detain, and forcibly return refugees to the terror, persecution, and murder in El Salvador and Guatemala.

We believe that justice and mercy require that people of conscience actively assert our God-given right to aid anyone fleeing from persecution and murder. The current administration of the United States law prohibits us from sheltering these refugees from Central America. Therefore we believe that administration of the law is immoral as well as illegal.

We beg of you, in the name of God, to do justice and love mercy in the administration of your office. We ask that "extended voluntary departure" be granted to refugees from Central America and that current deportation proceedings against these victims be stopped.

Until such time, we will not cease to extend the sanctuary of the church to undocumented people from Central America. Obedience to God requires this of us all.[5]

According to Rev. Fife, then, his conscience forced him to break one unjust law in order to uphold the integrity of a conflicting law, the Refugee Act of 1980.[6] Passed in order to bring U.S. immigration law into agreement with the 1967 United Nations Protocol Relating to the Status of Refugees,[7] the Act prohibits deportation of aliens back to countries where their "life or freedom would be threatened."[8]

If the Department of Justice and the Immigration and Naturalization Service somehow failed to notice Fife's letter, he continued to publicize his deliberate law breaking by holding a public ceremony, to which the press was invited, at which he actually presented one of the Salvadorans his church was hiding.[9] During a similar ceremony at the Wellington Avenue United Church of Christ of Chicago, Illinois, Reverend Michael McConnell boldly declared that "We cry 'Enough!'. . . We break the law and say, 'Enough to injustice!'"[10] Several other "sanctuary churches" also staged such ceremonies.[11]

In the face of such flagrant violations of the law, neither the INS nor DOJ at first took any legal action against the sanctuary workers. At least officially, they did not appear to view the Movement as a serious problem. In 1982, when the Movement was in its infancy, the Assistant General Counsel for the INS, Bill Joyce, downplayed its importance and implied that his agency sought to avoid a conflict with the church:

> We're not about to send investigators into a church and start dragging people out in front of the TV cameras. We'll just wait them out, wait until they leave the church. This is just a political thing that the churches are dreaming up to get publicity—a game to pressure the government to allow Salvadorans to stay here. If we thought it was a significant problem, then maybe we'd take a look at it. But there are plenty of illegal aliens out there.[12]

In 1983, the INS still held essentially the same position. David Ilchert, Northern California District Director of the INS, stated:

> We are not seeking a confrontation with church groups. The major thrust of the INS enforcement is

directed toward illegal aliens holding well-paying jobs that go to U.S. citizens or lawful residents. We go to work sites, not into neighborhoods, into homes or churches. The fact that some minister may call us up and say that some alien is living in his church, sleeping in his pew, would be a low priority for us.[13]

Even in the beginning of 1984, the INS continued to claim that the Sanctuary Movement actually was not as threatening as it seemed. One INS spokesman asserted that, "When you put it into perspective, the sanctuary movement is really not that big and is receiving an unjustified amount of attention."[14]   At least after 1981, it seems that the INS might have even issued an administrative order prohibiting its agents from looking for aliens in churches, schools, or hospitals.[15]

The INS's totally hands-off policy changed slightly when Border Patrol agents stopped a car full of sanctuary workers and undocumented aliens in February of 1984. The INS later charged the driver, Stacey Merkt, with "conspiring to transport and move, and transporting and moving two illegal aliens within the United States."[16]   A federal jury found her guilty, but on appeal the U.S. Court of Appeals for the Fifth Circuit reversed her conviction on the grounds of an erroneous jury instruction and remanded the case back to the district court for a retrial.[17]   Federal prosecutors later decided not to retry her and so dismissed the indictment.[18]   Even though the INS arrested and indicted Merkt, making her the first sanctuary worker prosecuted (the Border Patrol had arrested two sanctuary workers under similar circumstances in March of 1983, but had released them a few hours later without bringing charges),[19] the INS probably did not arrest her simply because she belonged to the Sanctuary Movement, but rather because they just happened to stop her car in a routine inspection for illegal aliens. Once she had been arrested and charged, the INS would have looked more foolish if it had released her after discovering that she was a sanctuary worker than if it had continued to prosecute her despite her religious motivation. The INS, after all, did not arrest Merkt in a church where she might have claimed "sanctuary," but in her car on a public road. Merkt's arrest, then, does not seem to signal the beginning of the government's intentional prosecution of the Sanctuary Movement. After the Movement's supporters made her into a martyr for human rights, and Amnesty International named her a "prisoner of conscience,"[20] the INS probably wished it had never arrested her.

The arrest of John Elder, director of the sanctuary shelter "Casa Romero," on April 13, 1984, also seems more like a chance arrest than a premeditated attempt to prosecute sanctuary workers. On March 12, Elder had driven three undocumented Salvadorans from the Casa Romero to a bus station in Harlington, Texas, six miles away. When Elder arrived at the bus station, INS agents watched the three Salvadorans get out of his car. The agents immediately arrested the three and recorded the license plate number of the car. After a check of the license plate number traced the car back to Elder,[21] the INS asked him to surrender voluntarily, a request which he refused.[22] On April 12, federal marshals went to the Casa Romero to arrest him, but the sight of "worshippers" and the press waiting for them apparently persuaded them to come back another day.[23] On April 13, they returned to the Casa and, after having the three undocumented Salvadorans identify Elder, arrested him on charges of illegally transporting undocumented aliens.[24] At trial, however, the jury acquitted Elder, finding that the prosecution had not proved that he had helped the Salvadorans to break immigration laws by driving them to the bus terminal.[25] Once again, therefore, the INS probably prosecuted a sanctuary worker more by accident then by intentionally looking for a member of the Sanctuary Movement.

Beginning in December of 1984, however, the INS appears to have begun specifically targeting sanctuary workers for prosecution. First the INS had a federal grand jury indict Merkt and Elder once again. The indictment of December 4 charged them with various counts of transporting and conspiracy to transport illegal aliens. A federal petit jury found Merkt not guilty of transporting but guilty of conspiracy. Judge Filomen Vela sentenced her to 179 days of prison, followed by nine months of probation.[26] After the Court of Appeals for the Fifth Circuit affirmed the decision of the district court,[27] Merkt and Elder petitioned the Supreme Court for certiorari, but their petition was denied.[28] Merkt then began serving her sentence at Fort Worth Federal Penitentiary on January 29, 1987. Probably because she was by then six-months pregnant, on April 17 Merkt was allowed to complete her sentence under house arrest.[29] The federal jury found Elder guilty of all charges, and he was sentenced to 150 days in a halfway house, which he began serving in April of 1985.[30] After having served 133 days, Elder was released on August 19 for good conduct.[31]

If *United States v. Jack Elder and Stacey Merkt* was the INS's preliminary poke at the Sanctuary Movement, *U.S. v. Aguilar, et al.* was its swift uppercut. The 71-count indictment against 16 sanctuary workers[32] came after a controversial undercover operation, "Operation Sojourner," in which the INS and DOJ paid former alien smugglers thousands of dollars and offered them immunity from prosecution in exchange for infiltrating churches and then spying on the sanctuary workers they found there.[33] The INS was apparently trying to prosecute the leaders of the Movement since those indicted included co-founders James Corbett and Rev. John Fife. But the INS did not overlook other prominent clergy in the Movement either; Sisters Darlene Nicgorski, Mary Waddell, Anna Priester, and Fathers Antonio Clark and Ramon Dagoberto Quiñones also found their names on the indictment. The list concluded with Phillip Conger and Katherina Flaherty, both from the Tucson Ecumenical Council Task Force on Central America; Peggy Hutchinson, from Tucson's Methodist Metropolitan Ministries; Cecilia del Carmen Juarez de Emery and Bertha Marthel-Benavidez, both Salvadorans living in Phoenix; Maria del Socorro Pardo de Aquilar, a Mexican national; and Wendy LeWin, Mary Kay Espinosa, and Nena MacDonald, three sanctuary volunteers. The prosecution also had 49 "refugees" throughout the country named "illegal alien unindicted co-conspirators" and subpoenaed 25 other sanctuary workers as "unindicted co-conspirators" to testify under immunity.[34]

Soon after the arraignment, Flaherty,[35] Emery and Martel-Benavidez plea-bargained for reduced charges, and the government dropped Priester and Waddell from the indictment due to Priester's supposedly poor health.[36] After a six-month trial,[37] the jury acquitted Corbett, Espinosa, and MacDonald, and found the other eight defendants guilty.[38] During sentencing, Hutchinson, Nicgorski, Conger (also known as Willis-Conger),[39] de Aguilar, Quinoñes, and Fife all received five years' probation, and Clark and LeWin received three years' probation.[40] As of November of 1987, all eight had appealed their convictions to the U.S. Court of Appeals for the Ninth Circuit and were awaiting decisions.[41] As of

October 1987, no other sanctuary workers had been indicted.[42]

Even though a few of them were given prison sentences, it seems that many members of the Sanctuary Movement were actually trying to provoke the government into prosecuting them, or at least were not completely sorry that they had been prosecuted. First, as noted above, the Sanctuary Movement's founders publicly announced that they were breaking the law, and even sent a signed confession to the Attorney General of the United States. In books such as *Sanctuary: The New Underground Railroad*[43] and *Sanctuary: A Resource Guide for Understanding and Participating in the Central American Refugees' Struggle,*[44] and in *¡Basta!,* the newsletter of the Chicago Religious Task Force on Central America,[45] sanctuary leaders more or less openly state that their religious convictions compel them to break U.S. immigration law, and in these publications they even urge others to break the law. Considering that the Chicago Religious Task Force on Central America publicly distributes a list, updated monthly, of the names, addresses, and telephone numbers of the sanctuaries throughout the country,[46] the government's undercover operation seems all the more superfluous.

Sanctuary organizers also provoked the government to react by having "caravans" of up to 100 cars, all full of sanctuary workers and undocumented Central Americans, travel across the country. One caravan passed through Washington, D.C., and sanctuary workers demonstrated in front of the INS's building at 425 I St., to the obvious chagrin of the INS's national staff.[47,48] The vehicles usually carried signs such as "Refugee Express," "Freedom Train," and "INS Stop Deportations." The 143 drivers and passengers of one caravan signed a statement saying that "We, the undersigned, are transporting undocumented

Salvadoran and Guatemalan refugees to the Freedom Seder at Temple Emanu-El"[49] in Tucson, Arizona.[50] The members of one caravan from Los Angeles to Chicago took the time to protest U.S. policy in Central America by entering Camp Pendleton, where a "battalion of marines" promptly arrested them. In Tacoma, Seattle, and Olympia (WA), Albuquerque (NM), San Francisco (CA), and East Lansing (MI), activists prayed and staged sit-ins at the INS's headquarters and other federal buildings to protest the arrests of Merkt and Elder.[51]

Many sanctuary workers, including those prosecuted, explain how the prosecutions have actually strengthened the Movement and emphasize that the Movement was indeed trying to confront the government. For example, Elder, just before his trial, said:

I'm looking for a confrontation. Not to be self-righteous about it, but there's a moral force behind what we're doing that has the potential to focus some light on foreign policy. They [the administration] refuse to look at the deeper issues. There's a war going on in El Salvador now; there are bombing raids financed by the U.S. government. This is the issue people are fleeing from. . . . One reason I don't feel that uncomfortable facing a possible fifteen-year sentence is because the stakes are the future lives of kids and women in El Salvador.[52]

During her trial, Darlene Nicgorski also commented that the government's prosecution of the Movement helped it by providing national publicity:

Whatever the verdict, if the government's intention was to intimidate, to stop the movement, it has failed.

. . . In that sense, the government has already lost.
Even if some of us are convicted. Even if some of us
have to do some time.   We have spoken out and the
issues have reached a broader public. This backfired
on the government. Whatever the verdict, it's not the
end. It's just the beginning.[53]

In a speech she gave at the 1986 Annual National Legal
Conference on Immigration and Refugee Policy in
Washington, D.C., one of the sanctuary workers' defense
attorneys, Ellen Yaroshefsky of the Center for
Constitutional Rights, echoed Nicgorski's sentiments:

What has become clear is, even if there should be any
conviction in this case on any of the counts—we have
one conspiracy count, and we have some thirty other
counts left—that essentially sanctuary has won the
case. I say that because the trial has accomplished an
educational goal—the morality and legality of
sanctuary is discussed in communities throughout the
U.S. There seems to be public recognition that the
truth is not being presented in this trial, and people
throughout the country are disturbed and ask why it is
that the truth is being suppressed in our legal system.
. . . This prosecution has opened up new avenues for
discussion of the asylum process and INS procedures.
. . . This trial will probably help the judicial system
look more closely at asylum claims.[54]

Similarly, although Deborah Taylor, coordinator of the San
Diego Interfaith Task Force on Central America, noticed
that the trial in Tucson apparently persuaded some people in
southern California to stop housing undocumented Central
Americans, she feels that it has generated positive publicity

for the Movement and increased its ranks nationally. "More people are working to help. . . . The movement has been strengthened. Over 100 new churches have joined since the trial started," she says.[55] Having its leaders convicted of felonies, then, does not seem to have hurt the Movement too much. Those convicted seem almost glad to have been prosecuted, as if they had wanted to be tried for their sanctuary activities.

The INS, which seems to have exhibited great restraint in prosecuting only 18 of the estimated "80 to 100 thousand" sanctuary workers in the United States[56] (as of April 18, 1988, the Chicago Religious Task Force on Central America listed 410 churches, synagogues, or other organizations as "declared sanctuaries" for undocumented Central Americans),[57] seems to agree. The chief of the INS's Border Patrol in Tucson, Leon Ring, stated:

> This underground railroad—or the various church groups—wanted publicity. They were baiting us to overreact. Therefore, we have been deliberately very low-key.[58]

In their internal memoranda, the INS also seems to approach the Movement cautiously. A memorandum by the INS's Central Office Intelligence (COINT), for example, recommends nothing more harsh than "being able to demonstrate that we *have not ignored* the situation" [emphasis added].[59]

That the Sanctuary Movement's provocations probably helped push the government to prosecute them can be seen by comparing the Movement to other organizations that engage in similar activities, but who try not to publicize those of their activities which might be legally questionable. Many of these groups, though they do not consider themselves part of the "Sanctuary Movement," nevertheless knowingly harbor and conceal Central Americans whom the INS would consider "illegal aliens." All of these organizations are religious, most coming from mainline Christian denominations in the U.S. Combined, these relief agencies handle many more undocumented aliens than does the entire Sanctuary Movement. In contrast to those in the Sanctuary Movement, however, these agencies take few if any public stands against U.S. foreign policy in Central America or on the advisability of "civil disobedience."[60]

According to a spokeswoman for "Refugee Services,"[61] for example, sub-entities that her organization funds feed and shelter undocumented Central Americans throughout the United States. These sub-entities do not encourage those Central Americans undiscovered by the INS to apply for asylum because only rarely do they receive it, and those who do not are subsequently deported.[62] In fiscal year 1986, for example, the percentage of asylum requests that the INS approved compared to those they denied was 4.6% for Salvadorans, 2.3% for Guatemalans, 0.0% for Hondurans, and 27.4% for Nicaraguans.[63] (Nicaraguans obviously have a much better chance of gaining asylum, especially since 1987, when the acceptance rate shot up to close to 85%.)[64] According to Refugee Services' Ms. Doe, while the Sanctuary Movement helps "hundreds" of undocumented aliens, organizations such as hers help "thousands." Although her organization supports the "right to decide to participate in the Sanctuary Movement," it does not openly support the Movement itself. The agency also avoids all public stands on sheltering "illegals." They do not, for example, call press conferences and parade "illegals" before television cameras. As Ms. Doe remarked, "You can't help [the undocumented aliens] and take public stands" too. Many of the sub-entities also refuse to make public statements about U.S. foreign policy in Central America.[65] To the best of my knowledge, none of these religious organizations has ever been prosecuted for harboring illegal aliens.[66]

At least one of the Tucson defendants seems to agree with this analysis. Sister Darlene Nicgorski commented after the trial that "If we had gone on helping refugees quietly, I don't think we would have been indicted."[67] And the Chicago Religious Task Force's Michael McConnell notes that the INS was specifically monitoring the amount of publicity the Sanctuary Movement received.[68] He also sees *United States v. Aguilar, et al.* as "a political trial from the beginning, aimed at stopping the Movement from effectively challenging U.S. immigration policy." Non-political relief agencies which do essentially the same things as the Sanctuary Movement, he claims, have not been prosecuted.[69]

As McConnell noted, and in sharp contrast to Refugee Services and similar organizations, many members of the Sanctuary Movement openly take political stands against U.S. foreign policy. The Chicago Religious Task Force on Central America proclaims in its "Statement of Faith" that:

> For us, to love is to create a movement capable of stopping U.S. intervention in Central America, a movement not simply of protest or witness but of resistance. This effort is profoundly religious and inevitably political.[70]

And according to a reviewer in *Monthly Review*, a Marxist political journal, sanctuary leaders Renny Golden and Michael McConnell hold that the Sanctuary Movement should "publicly declare that its intention is to stop U.S. intervention in Central America," and to build a "widespread resistance movement to U.S. imperialism." The reviewer ends her article by saying that "[i]f Marxists are searching for how to combine theory *with action,* they might start by reading this book" [emphasis in original], Golden and McConnell's *Sanctuary: The New Underground Railroad.*[71] When asked about this characterization of his book, McConnell did not object, saying that the reviewer was particularly accurate in emphasizing the "action" aspect of the Movement. He also noted that some sanctuary workers were liberation theologians.[72]

In their book, McConnell and Golden themselves admit to political aims. They begin by quoting Elliott Abrams, a former Assistant Secretary of State for Human Rights and Humanitarian Affairs and then Assistant Secretary of State for Inter-American Affairs,[73] who commented, "I think that many of the militants, let me put it that way, the militant activists, are really just opposing American policy in El Salvador." They also mention that the INS's Alan Nelson noted that "Most of the leaders are candid in acknowledging that the thrust of their movement is to oppose U.S. foreign policy in Central America." To these charges, Golden and McConnell agree: "Abrams and Nelson are correct in stating that the sanctuary movement has understood its faith stance on behalf of refugees as an inevitably political act."[74] Elsewhere in their book the authors show various Marxist leanings. They criticize "American liberals" for being "gradualists" opposing "violent" solutions, ignoring "historical analysis" and "structural oppression," and fearing to align themselves with "Central Americans involved in liberation struggles."[75] They conclude by discussing the "temptation of not considering a revolutionary process authentic unless it bears the label 'Christian,'"[76] and quoting a line from the "message to the

Tricontinental" given by "Che" Guevara,[77] the Latin
American revolutionary.

Not all sanctuary workers are equally left-wing or
equally political, of course. Co-founder Jim Corbett, for
one, opposes the views of Golden and McConnell, especially
their implied argument for revolutionary violence in order
to overthrow the current Central American regimes. "[A]ll
causes to which life must be sacrificed are among Moloch's
[the ancient Semitic god to whom children were sacrificed]
many names. He delights most in sacrifices that give him
the name of a good cause," Corbett argues.[78] He notes the
inhumanity of some in the Movement who put political
ideals above humanitarian or moral ones. One sanctuary
group, for example, was sent a Guatemalan couple that had
been forced to flee from leftists guerrillas who were
"murdering whole villages" during the civil war. But,
finding that the couple "lacked a correct political analysis
and were therefore unsuitable for sanctuary," the group had
the couple sent back to Tucson, and the two eventually
ended up talking to government interrogators back in
Guatemala.[79] Corbett ends with a scathing castigation of
Golden's and McConnell's views:

> When Jesus says we meet him in the poor and
> oppressed, I now have difficulty thinking of him as
> politically informed;   he always looks like that
> [Guatemalan] couple. Partisans who say that sanctuary
> must be political rather than apolitically humanitarian
> mean, precisely, that sanctuary services should be
> extended only to those among the oppressed who serve
> the cause of the oppressed, as determined by a correct
> political analysis. When they say that a sanctuary
> network that refuses to restrict itself in this way just
> wants to do refugee charity while ignoring the root

cause, they are simply saying that the sanctuary network is refusing to be guided by a political analysis that mandates these restrictions. Like his good and holy names, Moloch's correct political analyses are, of course, legion.[80]

Thus, although not all sanctuary workers are politically motivated, enough are to support the argument that the government was more disturbed by the Sanctuary Movement's politics than by its religion.

Indeed, if the government felt that the leaders of the Movement were more subject to political motivations and the lower levels mainly motivated by religion, their strike at the Tucson defendants might be seen more as an attack on political dissent rather than as a quashing of religious civil disobedience. The Western Regional Commissioner of the INS, Harold Ezell, seems to view the Sanctuary Movement in just such a fashion:

Q: *Would you please outline your stand on the sanctuary movement?*
A: The sanctuary issue is a Trojan horse. Outwardly it sounds so wonderful. How could you love God and not care for these people? That's a front. It's a Trojan horse, because on the inside the leadership that I'm talking about are very, very political. They are political activists doing everything they can to change the international foreign policy of the Reagan administration in Latin America, particularly in two countries, El Salvador and Guatemala. They don't talk about Nicaragua. In Nicaragua, seven of the nine bishops in the Catholic Church have stated, "We don't have any religious freedom here. There are no human rights anymore." My dad, Dr. Herb Ezell, pastor of

Harbor Christian Center in Wilmington, California, keeps giving me names of persons and churches who are being persecuted in Nicaragua. The Marxist-Leninist philosophy is being espoused there. There are many followers of sanctuary movement [sic]— particularly little churches around the country—who are misguided. Many are misled intentionally by the leaders of sanctuary movement [sic].

Q. *So it's not really a Christian issue, but a political one?*

A. That's right. That's why the trial in Tucson concerning the sanctuary movement smuggling illegal immigrants was a matter of law versus lawlessness. These are the issues, not church versus state.[81]

Thus, if the government sees only the leaders as highly political, it appears to have left alone most of the rank-and-file sanctuary workers who are motivated exclusively by religion. Breaking the law for purely religious reasons would seem to be almost permissible, in the government's view.

A comparison of the sentences the sanctuary workers received in federal district court with recent sentencing trends provides still more evidence showing the government's leniency toward offenders in the Sanctuary Movement; for of the six sanctuary workers convicted of violating 8 U.S.C. § 1324, the mean prison sentence was 0.71 months. Yet the mean sentence for the total population of 801 people convicted under this statute from June 30, 1984, to June 30, 1986, is 12.92 months, more than 18 times longer. Since F=3.21 for an analysis of variance (ANOVA) test at a confidence level of 95%, this large difference in means would appear to be statistically significant. For

further information on these statistics, see Appendix A
(Sentencing of Sanctuary Workers).[82]

If the government has treated the Sanctuary Movement
leniently, and it appears that it has, then the Movement's
religious affiliations would seem a likely reason for this
leniency. Indeed, INS officials have admitted their fear of
pressing the church too hard, of making themselves look
ridiculous by appearing to "persecute" religious people.
Bill Joyce, the Assistant General Counsel of the INS,
maintained that "We're not about to send some investigators
into a church and start dragging people out in front of the
TV cameras."[83] Another INS spokesperson claimed that the
INS was not "seeking a confrontation with church groups,"
and wondered about the motives of "these good religious
people." And although Bill Johnson from the Tucson INS
office asserts that "it means nothing that the driver" of a car
carrying an illegal alien "wears a Roman Catholic collar,"[84]
Tucson's Border Patrol chief, Leon Ring, feels differently
about churches:

> Certain arrests could have taken place if we wanted to,
> but we felt that the government would end up looking
> ridiculous, especially as far as going into church
> property—anything where the ethics involved would
> be questioned.[85]

Finally, Border Patrol agent Thomas Martin wrote just
after observing Fife's public "ceremony of sanctuary" that:

> It seems that this movement is more political than
> religious, but that a ploy is going to be Border Patrol
> "baiting" by that group in order to demonstrate to the
> public that the U.S. government via it's [sic] jack-
> booted gestapo Border Patrol Agents think [sic]

nothing of breaking down the doors of their churches
to drag Jesus Christ out to be tortured and murdered.
I believe that all political implications should be
considered before any further action is taken toward
this group.[86]

The Sanctuary Movement's religious motivations, then,
seem to have given pause to the INS.

*   *   *   *   *   *

It appears that the INS's fear of strong support for the
Sanctuary Movement was not without foundation. Nor are
the Movement's supporters insignificant. Just before
sentencing in the Tucson trial, for example, 47 members of
Congress, led by Representatives Morris Udall and Joseph
Moakley, took the unusual step of writing to Judge Earl
Carroll and urging him to "consider the underlying
circumstances in Central America and humanitarian motives
of the defendants" when sentencing them.[87]

Many, if not most, American religious groups also
support the Movement. MacEoin lists as "national bodies
now on record as endorsers of the sanctuary movement" the
General Assembly of the reunited Presbyterian Church,
American Friends Service Committee, Clergy and Laity
Concerned, Church of the Brethren General Board,
National Assembly of Religious Women, Mennonite Central
Committee, National Coalition of American Nuns, United
Methodist Board of Church and Society, Unitarian
Universalist Service Committee, United Church of Christ
Office for Church and Society, Pax Christi, Board of
National Ministries of the American Baptist Church,
Methodist Federation for Social Action, Commission on
Home Ministries of the General Conference Mennonite

Church, Immigration and Refugee Service of the Lutheran Council, and the National Federation of Priests' Councils.[88] In the Catholic community, Archbishops Raymond Hunthausen and Rembert Weakland, and Bishops Joseph Fiorensa, John Fitzpatrick, Manuel Moreno, Thomas O'Brien, and Jerome Hastrich, as well as the Maryknoll Order and many of the Franciscans and Redemptorists have all pledged their support for the Movement.[89] By some accounts, the Pope may even approve.[90]

According to supporters such as Gary MacEoin, sanctuary is no less politically "ecumenical":

Contrary to administration claims, supporters of sanctuary include representatives of all shades of the political spectrum, including prochoice people and antiabortionists, card-carrying Democrats and Republicans, "yuppies," welfare recipients, blacks, whites, Hispanics, business executives, students, educators, physicians, farmers, feminists. It is a Rainbow Coalition, the dream of Jesse Jackson (who, incidentally, is a strong supporter).[91]

To prove MacEoin's point, Reverend Ted Loder tells of a "businessman from Canton, Ohio," who, though a "staunch Reagan supporter," was "a leader in trying to get his church to declare Public Sanctuary," and was "taking a leave from his electrical contracting company to devote more time" to the Sanctuary Movement.[92]

Although few polls have extensively studied public opinion on the issue, those that do seem to indicate that the general public can at least tolerate the Movement. One poll of Maricopa County, Arizona, for example, found that 71% of those who were familiar with the Sanctuary Movement and believed that civil disobedience is sometimes justified felt that sanctuary workers were correct in violating U.S.

immigration law. Overall, however, only 33% agreed with the Movement.[93] Unfortunately, it appears that no nation-wide survey on this subject exists.

Sanctuary's few prominent opponents include *The Arizona Republic*,[94] the National Association of Evangelicals, Catholic Bishop Anthony Bevilacqua,[95] lobbyists for immigration control, like Patrick Burns of the Federation for Immigration Reform,[96] and obviously parts of the INS and the Reagan Administration. On the whole, however, Sanctuary's opponents seem drowned out by its more numerous or more vocal advocates.

Protected by its powerful friends, the Sanctuary Movement has been almost coddled by the federal government despite the Reagan Administration's disdain. Neither the religious practices of its members nor their religiously inspired actions on behalf of Central Americans seem "extreme" or dangerous. They therefore "deserve" the lenient treatment that they received. Religion, it seems, is sometimes an acceptable excuse for breaking the law.

Notes

1.   Administrative Office of the United States Courts, Statistical Analysis and Reports Division, *United States District Courts Sentences Imposed Chart, Twenty-Four Month Period Ended June 30, 1986* (Washington, D.C.: Government Printing Office, 1987), p. 6.

2.   Gary MacEoin, "A Brief History of the Sanctuary Movement," in Gary MacEoin, ed., *Sanctuary: A Resource Guide for Understanding and Participating*

in the Central American Refugees' Struggle (San Francisco, CA: Harper & Row, 1985), pp. 19-22.

3.   John M. Fife, "The Sanctuary Movement," *Church and Society*, March/April 1985, p. 19, in MacEoin, pp. 19-20.

4.   MacEoin, p. 21.

5.   Letter to William French Smith from the Reverend John M. Fife, March 23, 1982, in MacEoin, pp. 21-22.

6.   Pub. L. No. 96-212, 94 Stat. 102.

7.   Ignatius Bau, *This Ground is Holy: Church Sanctuary and Central American Refugees* (Mahwah, NJ: Paulist Press, 1985), p. 55.

8.   8 U.S.C. § 1253(h)(1).

9.   MacEoin, p. 22.

10.   Bau, p. 218.

11.   Ibid., pp. 22-23.

12.   Ibid., pp. 87-88.

13.   Ibid., p. 88.

14.   Ibid., p. 89.

15.   Ibid., pp. 75 & 218.

16.   *United States v. Merkt*, 764 F.2d 266, 268 (1985).

17.   764 F.2d 266 & 268.

18.   *United States v. Merkt* [and Elder], 794 F.2d 950, 962 (1986), footnote 12.

19.   Bau, pp. 79-80.

20.   "Sanctuary Movement Member is Prisoner of Conscience," *Amnesty International Newsletter,* vol. XVII, no. 4, p. 7.

21.   *United States v. Elder,* 601 F. Supp. 1574, 1576 (1985).

22.   Bau, p. 80.

23.   Ibid., p. 219.

24.   Ibid., p. 80; and 601 F. Supp. at 1576.

25.   Bau, p. 81.

26.   Ibid., pp. 82-83.

27.   794 F.2d 950.

28.   *Merkt v. United States,* 107 S. Ct. 1603 (1987).

29.   "Sanctuary Movement Member is Prisoner of Conscience," p. 7; and "House Arrest for Sanctuary Worker in USA," *Amnesty International Newsletter,* vol. XVII, no. 6, p. 7.

30.   Bau, p. 83.

31.   Arizona Sanctuary Defense Fund, "Historical Highlights of the Sanctuary Movement," p. 4, in United Methodist Church, General Board of Global

Ministries, National Program Division, *Sanctuary: A Ministry of Assistance and Solidarity* (New York, NY: United Methodist Church, 1986).

32. Bau, p. 83.

33. Sandy Tolan and Carol Ann Bassett, "Operation Sojourner: Informers in the Sanctuary Movement," *The Nation,* vol. 241, July 20/27, 1985, pp. 40-41.

34. Bau, pp. 84-85.

35. Arizona Sanctuary Defense Fund, p. 4.

36. Bau, p. 87.

37. Bill Curry, "8 of 11 Activists Guilty in Alien Sanctuary Case: Defiant Group Says 6-Month Trial Hasn't Ended Movement to Help Central American Refugees," *Los Angeles Times,* May 2, 1986, part I, p. 1.

38. Ibid., p. 18.

39. Bau, p. 84.

40. Bill Curry, "Five Activists Put on Probation," *Los Angeles Times,* July 2, 1986, part I, p. 12; and Bill Curry, "INS to Study Claims of Abuse as Sanctuary Sentencing Ends," *Los Angeles Times,* July 3, 1986, part I, p. 4.

41. Office of the Clerk, U.S. Court of Appeals for the Ninth Circuit, San Francisco, CA, interview by telephone with author, November 24, 1987.

42. Michael McConnell of the Chicago Religious Task Force on Central America, interview by telephone with author, October 30, 1987.

43. Renny Golden and Michael McConnell, *Sanctuary: The New Underground Railroad* (Maryknoll, NY: Orbis Books, 1986).

44. MacEoin, op. cit..

45. "Sanctuary and the Central American Crisis: Selected Resources," p. 1, in United Methodist Church.

46. Chicago Religious Task Force on Central America, "Declared Sanctuaries (Nationwide), January 1986," in United Methodist Church.

47. Golden, pp. 70-71.

48. Allen Anderson and the United States Immigration and Naturalization Service, Central Office Intelligence (COINT), "Strategic Assessment: The Sanctuary Movement," internal memorandum, December 1983, point 16; obtained in response to Freedom of Information request of April 24, 1986, by Dr. Michael D. Roe, 397 Sherburne Ave., St. Paul, MN 55103.

49. Golden, pp. 70-71.

50. Chicago Religious Task Force.

51. Golden, pp. 70-71.

52. Ibid., pp. 68-69.

53. Bill Curry, "Sanctuary Jury Ends 7th Day Without Verdict," *Los Angeles Times,* April 30, 1986, part I, p. 12.

54. Ellen Yaroshefsky, "The Tucson Trial and its Legal Consequences for Asylum Seekers," in Lydio F. Tomasi, ed., *In Defense of the Alien,* vol. IX, Proceedings of the 1986 Annual National Legal Conference on Immigration and Refugee Policy (New York, NY: Center for Migration Studies, 1987), p. 180.

55. Miriam Davidson, "Sanctuary Workers Active, But Cautious: Tucson Trial Has Caused Apprehension, But Hasn't Stifled Zeal," *Christian Science Monitor,* March 12, 1986, p. 8.

56. Bau, pp. 75-87.

57. McConnell, interview by telephone with author, April 18, 1988.

58. Bau, p. 89.

59. Anderson, point 22.

60. This paragraph is based on a telephone conversation of October 30, 1987, with Rev. Michael McConnell of the Chicago Religious Task Force on Central America, and on a telephone conversation of November 12, 1987, with "Ms. Doe," who wishes to remain anonymous for fear of causing any prosecutions against those relief centers funded by her religious relief organization, which I shall refer to as "Refugee Services."

61. Pseudonym, see above footnote.

62. Doe, see above.

63. U.S. Immigration and Naturalization Service, "Asylum Cases Filed with District Directors," fiscal year 1986, computer printout, Washington, D.C., October 1986.

64. U.S. Immigration and Naturalization Service, "Asylum Cases Filed with District Directors," fiscal year 1987 through September 1987, computer printout, Washington, D.C., October 1987.

65. Doe.

66. Ibid., and McConnell, October 30, 1987.

67. Rusty Brown, "Sister Darlene Nicgorski," *Ms.*, vol. 45, January 1987, p. 56.

68. McConnell, October 30, 1987, and Anderson.

69. McConnell, October 30, 1987.

70. Chicago Religious Task Force on Central America, "Statement of Faith," *¡Basta!*, Tucson edition, January 1985, p. IV, in Bau, p. 31.

71. Sheila D. Collins, "The New Underground Railroad," *Monthly Review*, vol. 38, no. 1, May 1986, pp. 1-7.

72. McConnell, April 18, 1988.

73. *Who's Who in America* (Wilmette, IL: MacMillan, 1986), 1986-87, 44th ed., vol. I, p. 7.

74. Golden, pp. 88-89.

75. Ibid., pp. 174-175.

76. Ibid., p. 178.

77. Ibid., p. 197.

78. Jim Corbett, "The Sanctuary Church," Pendle Hill Pamphlet 270 (Wallingford, PA: Pendle Hill Publications, 1986), p. 36.

79. Ibid., p. 37.

80. Ibid.

81. Harold Ezell, "A Call from the Wall," *Voice* (a publication of the Full Gospel Business Men's Fellowship International, P.O. Box 5050, Costa Mesa, CA 92628), vol. 34, no. 9, September 1986, pp. 11-12.

82. Data for the calculations in this paragraph came from Bau, p. 83; 794 F.2d 950; the "Active Criminal Docket" sheets for *U.S. v. Aguilar, et al.,* Case No. CR-85-00008-01 through -16, Clerk of the Court, U.S. District Court (Phoenix, AZ); and the *Sentences Imposed Chart* for 1984-86 cited above. The amount of prison time, probation time, and/or fine that each defendant received was entered as one row of data in the MINITAB statistics program on a VAX mainframe computer. Where a felon received no prison time, the amount of time entered in the "prison" column was 0, and a similar procedure was followed for the "probation" and "fine" columns. For purposes of these calculations, John Elder's sentence to a halfway house was considered a prison sentence. The "prison" columns were then compared using the "AOVONEWAY" command in MINITAB to calculate the means and 95% confidence intervals for both the total population and the sanctuary workers, as well as to figure "F" for the ANOVA test of similarity between two populations.

83.   Bau, p. 87.

84.   Ibid., p. 88.

85.   Ibid., p. 89.

86.   Tolan, p. 43.

87.   Lee May, "47 in Congress Write to Judge, Ask Leniency in Sanctuary Case," *Los Angeles Times,* July 1, 1986, part I, p. 14.

88.   MacEoin, pp. 25-26.

89.   Ibid., pp. 27-28.

90.   David Maroniss and Loren Jenkins, "Pope Backs Sheltering Immigrants, Sanctuary Movement Virtually Endorsed at Mass in Texas," *Washington Post,* September 14, 1987, p. A1.

91.   MacEoin, p. 25.

92.   Ted Loder, "Reflections," in Loder, *No One But Us: Personal Reflections On Public Sanctuary* (San Diego, CA: LuraMedia, 1986).

93.   *The Arizona Republic* and *The Phoenix Gazette, Arizona Poll* (Phoenix, AZ), January 1985.

94.   *The* (Phoenix) *Arizona Republic,* editorial, March 31, 1987, in *Editorials on File,* vol. 18, 1987, p. 327.

95.   Bau, p. 188.

96.   May, p. 14.

Chapter III

The Reverend Moon's Trial for Tax Evasion

The Reverend Sun Myung Moon's trial for tax evasion illustrates the reaction of the public and the government to what they perceive as "extreme" religious beliefs and practices. Few complain about the humanitarian programs that Moon's Unification Church sponsors, but most Americans seem genuinely afraid of his supposedly "bizarre" religious beliefs and practices. They accuse him and his church of "brainwashing," "mind control," or worse. As the founder and leader of a major international "cult,"[1] Reverend Moon was almost universally despised at the time of his trial, and many continue to view him as an especially sinister threat to America's youth.

Seemingly because of this public hatred, the federal government treated Moon severely. At the apparent urging of one of Moon's powerful enemies in the U.S. Senate, the Internal Revenue Service targeted Moon's taxes for an audit, and the Department of Justice later obtained a conviction against him for tax fraud. In a prosecution and trial marked by probable irregularities, the Department of Justice interpreted the tax code in such a novel fashion that most American religious leaders later objected strongly to Justice's legal reasoning. Their support seems to have come too late, however, to save Rev. Moon from spending 18 months in prison.

* * * * * *

Every year on April 15, all Americans, whether rich, poor, or neither, must file their tax returns with the Internal Revenue Service. In 1981, for example, the IRS receive 166.5 million tax returns.[2] Most of the time, this process takes place more or less smoothly, with few serious complaints from either the taxpayer or the IRS.

Although the American system of tax collection must to a large extent be based on voluntary compliance (the IRS cannot possibly verify 166 million returns), occasionally the IRS does individually examine, or "audit," a taxpayer's return. Of the 166.5 million returns filed in 1981, the IRS examined 1.9 million, or about 1%.[3] Of this comparatively large number of taxpayers, only a miniscule fraction are ever investigated for possible criminal violations of the tax code. Again in 1981, the IRS investigated for possible criminal violations only 0.3% of all those audited, or only 0.003% of all taxpayers. Few of these investigations result in criminal charges being filed,[4] perhaps because of the difficulty of the IRS winning a trial for tax evasion; for not only must the government prove that the defendant actually did fail to pay federal income taxes, it must also prove "beyond a reasonable doubt" that the defendant "knowingly and willfully" defrauded the government.[5] "Honest mistakes," then, do not convict one of tax evasion; criminal intent is necessary as well. And given that tax lawyers often earn an additional LL.M. degree in tax law before practicing, and that a claim of "uncertainty" about the exceedingly complex tax code is sometimes a legitimate defense in trials for tax evasion,[6] "honest mistakes" would seem far from rare. Often the government is reluctant to bring charges of tax evasion because simply investigating cases of tax fraud can prevent further violations. As Sheldon S. Cohen, former Commissioner of the Internal

Revenue Service, puts it, "Generally, tax offenders who are discovered do not, and would not, repeat this offense, even if not ultimately indicted. . . . [F]or most people, the long ordeal of the investigation is punishment enough."[7]

It is hardly surprising, then, that in 1981 the IRS recommended that only 1,978 taxpayers be prosecuted, of which 1,152 pleaded guilty, 60 *nolo contendere,* and 282 were convicted after a trial. Of those sentenced in 1981, 49.7% received prison terms.[8] Assuming the percentage of those sentenced to jail in 1981 is representative of all the sentences of those convicted of or pleading guilty to tax violations that year, the percentage of taxpayers that went to jail for tax fraud was an almost negligible 0.0004%.

Yet amazingly enough, the Reverend Sun Myung Moon, the Korean founder and leader of the Unification Church, found himself in this extremely "select" group. For on May 18, 1982, a federal jury found him guilty of filing false tax returns and conspiracy to evade taxes, and he was later sentenced to 18 months in prison and "fined $25,000 plus costs."[9] His prison sentence of 18 months, moreover, puts him in the 69th percentile for all those sentenced from 1977-86 under 18 U.S.C. § 371, which carries the most severe penalty of all the statutes under which he was convicted.[10]

But the length of his sentence is not the only aspect of Moon's investigation and prosecution which sets him apart from most other taxpayers; for according to Senator Orrin Hatch, who held a hearing investigating the investigation and prosecution of Rev. Moon,[11] some lawyers at the Department of Justice were at first reluctant to prosecute the Korean clergyman:

> The three Justice Department attorneys who initially undertook an independent review of a possible

criminal action against Reverend Moon unanimously agreed, independently of each other, that there was no case.[12]

Senator Hatch also discovered other facts which militated against prosecution and made Moon's situation exceptional. According to "Washington, D.C. attorneys who had experience working for the Department of Justice,"[13] DOJ guidelines do not recommend prosecution if the amount of tax allegedly owed is sufficiently small:

> According to the Justice Department's review, Reverend Moon's tax liability, even if the government's case could be proven, was a mere $7,300 for a three year period [or an average of $2,433 per year]. I have been advised that the Justice Department's own guidelines state that criminal tax cases will not be brought if the alleged tax deficiency is less than $2,500 per year.[14]

An even more convincing point is that since Moon failed to take advantage of "a charitable tax deduction of approximately $700,000," one of the DOJ's attorney's argued that it would be "inconsistent to attempt to try an evasion charge [of $7,300] in the face of the $700,000 deduction."[15] Finally, Hatch noted that "[i]t simply makes no sense whatsoever" to argue that Moon would evade $7,300 in taxes when his "financial losses [from his newspaper *The Washington Times*] have exceeded $100 million over the past 3 years."[16]

According to a statement by Rev. Moon, which Senator Hatch's "inspection of the [DOJ's] prosecution memorandum . . . generally confirmed,"[17]

> the recommendations [of the three lower attorneys]
> then went up to a high-level, political appointee, with
> no criminal tax experience, who reversed all the
> recommendations of his own people, and authorized
> prosecution by the U.S. attorney in New York, without
> giving any good reason.[18]

Thus, despite all of the arguments not to prosecute, a
political appointee forced the case, making one suspect that
tax law was not the only basis for his or her decision.

On October 15, 1981,[19] the U.S. Attorney's Office filed
a 13-count indictment against Sun Myung Moon and his
Japanese associate, Takeru Kamiyama. The counts charged
them with conspiracy to file false federal income tax
returns, to obstruct justice, and to make false statements;
filing false tax returns for 1973, 1974, and 1975; and
perjury.[20]

The U.S. Court of Appeals for the Second Circuit
summarized the facts and main issues surrounding Moon's
trial as follows:

> The case focused principally on bank accounts
> held in Reverend Moon's name in the Park Avenue
> office of the Chase Manhattan Bank. On March 27,
> 1973 Reverend Moon walked into the Chase branch
> and opened a personal checking account and a savings
> account. During the next nearly three years over 1.7
> million dollars was [sic] deposited in these accounts in
> Moon's name, all but $200,000 of which was in cash.
> A substantial portion of the funds were [sic]
> transferred to high-yielding Chase time deposits held
> in Moon's name. During the years 1973-1975 these
> investments earned more than $100,000 in interest,

not reported as income on Moon's tax returns for the years in question. Also at issue was $50,000 worth of stock issued to Moon in 1973 in Tong II Enterprises, Inc., a corporation organized in New York in 1973 by Moon and Kamiyama which was engaged in the business of importing products from Korea. The receipt of this stock, which the government apparently views as a dividend, also was not reflected as income on Moon's tax return.

The critical issue is whether, as the government claims, Moon owned these assets and was therefore required to pay income taxes on the bank interest and the value of the stock or, as the defense urges, Moon held these assets merely beneficially or as a trustee for the Unification Church.[21]

To put the case very simply, if the Chase accounts and the Tong II stock actually belonged to the Unification Church, Moon would not have to pay taxes on them, but if they belonged to Moon personally, he would owe taxes on them, and would therefore be guilty of tax evasion for failing to report them as income.

From the beginning, the government tried to portray Moon as more of a "very, very successful businessman" than as the revered leader of a worldwide religion. The prosecution claimed that Moon acted as if the Chase accounts were "his money to do with as he pleased," and produced deposit slips and checks to support their assertion. Some money from the accounts had helped to pay for "personal items" like the Moon children's "private-school tuition," and a $361,000 estate in Irvington, New York.[22]

Moon's principal attorney, Charles Stillman, countered that the Korean evangelist "came here to preach for his movement. He didn't come here to cheat the United States out of his taxes." He affirmed that the account at the Chase Manhattan Bank contained only the Unification Church's money, that Moon served only as its trustee.[23]   Another attorney for the Unification Church, John Biermans, argues that:

> To a large extent these funds came from overseas Church members who felt more confident giving money directly to Rev. Moon than to the fledgling Unification Church in the United States which was not yet organized on a national basis at that time.[24]

According to Biermans, then, Moon kept the donations in a bank account in his own name only in his capacity as leader of the Unification Church, and not as a private citizen.

But perhaps the most convincing evidence indicating selective prosecution of Moon is that other religious leaders "have engaged in comparable conduct without being prosecuted":

> Specifically, Reverend Moon submitted evidence that officials and ministers of other churches hold church funds in accounts in their own names, and have discretion to spend such funds on some of their personal needs [as well as on] the needs of their churches, but have never been required to pay income taxes on the interest accrued on the corpus of such accounts nor have been prosecuted for not doing so.[25]

Later *amici curiae* briefs to the Supreme Court specified that many Catholic,[26] Baha'i, Mormon, Christian Scientist,

Jewish, and Episcopal clergy have held or continue to hold church property in their own name.[27]

On a more general level, two clergymen who have undoubtedly violated federal tax laws have thus far received much lighter treatment than did Moon. The IRS had been investigating Jim Bakker's "PTL Ministries" for years[28] and even recommended taking away its tax exemption for 1980-83,[29] yet it was only after news of Bakker's sex scandal that the government finally took him to court.[30] And even now, with Bakker in disgrace, some government investigators are "not enthusiastic" about prosecuting him.[31] The IRS also seems to have coddled the controversial Catholic Archbishop Raymond Hunthausen. After he refused to pay half of his federal income tax in protest over "our nation's continuing involvement in the race for nuclear arms supremacy,"[32] the IRS merely garnisheed his wages.[33]

With the Supreme Court as their last hope for overturning Moon's conviction, his lawyers filed for *certiorari* on January 26, 1984.[34] The support for their petition that began to flood in from the religious and civil liberties communities can only be described as overwhelming, even if it did seem to come too late to change Moon's fate. Among his religious supporters, the American Coalition of Unregistered Churches, Bishop Ernest Unterkoefler, Clare Boothe Luce, Eugene McCarthy, the Coalition of Catholic Laymen, the Church of Jesus Christ of Latter-Day Saints, the National Council of the Churches of Christ in the USA, the Presbyterian Church (USA), the American Baptist Churches in the USA, the African Methodist Episcopal Church, the National Association of Evangelicals, and the Southern Christian Leadership Conference all filed *amicus curiae* briefs for *certiorari* to the Supreme Court.[35] Individual clergy, including the Reverends Greg Dixon (Indianapolis Baptist

Temple),[36] Dean Kelly (National Council of Churches),[37] Tim LaHaye (American Coalition for Traditional Values),[38] Bob Grant (Christian Voice),[39] Joseph Lowery (Southern Christian Leadership Conference),[40] Donald Sills (Coalition for Religious Freedom),[41] and Jerry Falwell (Moral Majority),[42] also voiced their opposition to the government's prosecution of Rev. Moon. Nor were civil libertarians without a voice. *Amicus* briefs came from Religious Freedom International, the American Civil Liberties Union, Catholic League for Religious and Civil Rights, Coalition for Religious Freedom, Christian Legal Society, National Emergency Civil Liberties Committee, National Bar Association, and the Freemen Institute.[43]

   Few of Moon's "supporters" cared for his religion,[44] yet all felt obliged to defend him because of the legal precedent that his case was setting and its possible future application to themselves. As Colman McCarthy, a columnist for *The Washington Post,* put it:

> This is a Noah's Ark of views and styles. Everyone is on board, not to express faith in Moon but to perform the good works of protecting his right to express his Unification beliefs. If his church is under unfair attack this time, someone else's may be next time.[45]

So much did principle outweigh distaste for the defendant that even the Sparticist League, a Marxist-Leninist political organization, wrote an *amicus* brief for Moon,[46] an outspoken anti-communist.[47]

   Despite this tardy but massive support for Moon, the Supreme Court refused to hear his case.[48] Moon was thus condemned to spend 18 months of his life in a federal prison.

It seems likely that the federal government considered Moon's religious practices and the many accusations against him and his church when deciding whether to investigate and prosecute him for tax evasion. As Dr. Charles Rice, a professor at the University of Notre Dame Law School, puts it,

This is a case which involves, ultimately, I believe, a facet of the tendency to impose a state religion. The state is saying that only those religions which are within the parameters of approved doctrine and approved practice will be allowed to exist.[49]

Or more simply, enough Americans disliked Rev. Moon's religion strongly enough that they had him put in prison.

Even if most American religious leaders and civil libertarians defended Moon's *legal* position, the public in general and perhaps the religious leaders themselves seemed to abhor Moon and his church. Moon's attorneys, for instance, presented the following evidence of hostility to Moon:

two large boxes of newspaper clippings, all of which attacked Reverend Moon and the Unification faith; two books similarly hostile to the Church; reviews of a film then playing in Manhattan—"Ticket to Heaven"—which the *New York Daily News* described as "an indictment of the Unification Church"; and information concerning two separate instances where business concerns, linked only by rumor to Reverend Moon, were practically driven out of business by negative public reaction.[50]

Public opinion polls also indicate the dislike many feel towards Moon. When asked what effect "religious cults" have on the young people who join them, 53% of those surveyed responded that the "cults" have a "negative effect," 18% a "positive effect," 18% "no effect," and 11% "no opinion."[51]   Other surveys show downright fear of Moon. Of the respondents in another survey, for example, 69% thought that groups like "the Unification Church" were a "bad" influence, and 59% even found them "dangerous." Only 1% believed them to be an influence for "good."[52] Finally, "cults" in one poll topped the list of "groups not wanted as neighbors" at 44% of all surveyed.[53]   It seems that most Americans, then, both hate and fear Reverend Moon and his church.

Moon also had enemies in the U.S. Senate.   For the investigation of Moon was apparently prompted by a letter Senator Robert Dole of Kansas wrote to the Internal Revenue Service in January of 1976.   After receiving "a petition from 14,000 Kansans"[54] criticizing the alleged or real practices of the Unification Church, Senator Dole wrote to Donald Alexander, then the Commissioner of the IRS, questioning the Church's tax exemption:

> A large number of my constituents have contacted me about the Unification Church headed by Mr. Sun Myung Moon.   Their questions and statements raise doubt in my mind about the tax exempt status of that organization.[55]

Dole states that, as he understands tax law, "the first test for a tax exemption on religious grounds is that the group must be organized and operated exclusively for religious purposes,"[56] and then goes on to suggest that "a major goal [of the Unification Church] is the accumulation of wealth."

Dole also claims that "[s]ome statements by Mr. Moon and activities by some of his followers indicate a substantial political purpose."[57]

Dole even questions whether the Unification Church is indeed a "religion":

> Most of those contacting me question whether the organization is based *on bona fide religion or on mind control techniques.* Parents of members and former members state that while initial entry into the group is clearly voluntary, the subsequent actions of members suggest the loss of any ability to make any reasoned or unguided choice about continued participation in the group. This may indicate that the organization is maintained *not by religious motivation,* but by the calculated eradication or erosion of each member's ability to make an alternate choice. The well-documented process of training and initiation activities appears to substantiate *that the organization is based more on mind control and indoctrination than on religious faith.*[58] [Emphasis added.]

The Senator thus criticizes two mainly religious activities of the Church, its proselytizing and "discipleship."

His letter concludes by calling for an investigation of the Church:

> Based on the facts reported by my constituents and by articles in the public media, it appears that the tax exempt status of the Unification Church is questionable. It is my feeling, on this basis, that an audit of the organization may be warranted.[59]

Although the IRS might have investigated Moon and his church without prodding from Dole, the Senator's prominent position in national affairs makes his recommendation seem at least very influential, especially as seen through the eyes of the IRS. In 1976, when he urged the IRS to audit Moon, Dole served on the Senate Committee on Budget and the Subcommittee on Administration of the Internal Revenue Code of the Senate Committee on Finance.[60] On the national scene, he was running for Vice-President on the Republican ticket.[61] By 1981, when Dole was seemingly urging the DOJ to prosecute Moon, he had risen to the post of chairman of the Senate Finance Committee, and also served on its Subcommittee on Oversight of the Internal Revenue Service.[62] If the IRS would listen to anyone in Congress, it probably would have been Robert Dole.   And, as cases such as *Bob Jones University v. United States*[63] have shown, the IRS's tax exemption division will sometimes let politics influence whom it chooses to audit.

Just one month after he wrote the letter to the IRS, Dole held an "Information Meeting" on the "cults," which, he latter admitted, "wasn't a totally balanced meeting. We heard from frustrated parents by the thousands who were looking for a little balance in the Congress of the United States."[64] By holding such a "meeting," Dole might have been trying to give the IRS even more reasons to audit Moon.

Dole continued to express his opposition to, or at least deep suspicion of, "religious cults" like the Unification Church by holding a second hearing, the "Information Meeting on the Cult Phenomenon in the United States" on February 5, 1979.[65] Coming just after the Jonestown/People's Temple Massacre in Guyana, the meeting often became highly charged, with much applause, booing, and extemporaneous remarks from the audience.[66] Although not necessarily done intentionally, until just a few days before the hearing the balance of the witnesses apparently was heavily "anti-cult."[67]   The hearing's organizers absolutely refused to allow at least one potentially damaging pro-Unification Church witness to speak.[68] Only after a last-minute effort by an ecumenical coalition of American religious leaders, including representatives of the Unification Church,[69] to balance the proceedings did Senator Dole and his colleagues schedule any "strong advocates for religious liberty" or any other witnesses that did not "have definite positions in support of regulation of 'cult' activity or efforts to 'deprogram' members of such groups."[70] At the very least, then, Senator Dole's actions indicate that he harbors some suspicion, if not outright hostility, to the religious practices of groups like the Unification Church.

Many witnesses in Dole's second "Information Meeting" called for the government to act against the "cults." Although a few of the witnesses claimed not to be "talking about any new group's religious beliefs," their pleas for "medical and legal intervention and an ambitious campaign of public information" to distinguish "between *a legitimate religion and a cult*"[71] [emphasis added] seem to indicate that those groups they labelled "cults," including the Unification Church,[72] were by definition not "legitimate religions."   Thus, if "cults" were not true religions, their members did not have any true religious beliefs to be protected from governmental intrusion. These witnesses did not even mention protecting such groups' religious *practices*, which they would probably classify as "dangerous form[s] of physical and emotional abuse" or "the systematic destruction of the individual and his human right to freedom of thought."[73]

Dr. John Clark, a professor from Harvard Medical School who had researched "subject conversions," also called for governmental action against "absolutist groups," asserting that "the level of public nuisance is now so high that both scientists and public servants must react strongly before it is too late," and added that "the responsibility for the acts of the members is clearly with the leaders."[74] Dr. Clark's remarks, then, seem to point to Rev. Moon, the "leader" of a "religious cult," as a prime target for the government's action.

One witness even specified how and at what level the government should move against the "cults"—prosecute them at the national level:

> There are existing statutes under which many of America's cults may already be prosecuted. We have come here today to request direct action at the national level to counter this growing threat of mind control.[75]

Given the stridency of such requests, it seems possible that Senator Dole called the 1979 meeting to make it appear as though the "experts" were demanding the next phase of Moon's tax case: his indictment and prosecution for tax evasion.

Once the IRS had finished their investigation, the case was assigned to Martin Flumenbaum, then an Assistant U.S. Attorney in the Southern District of New York,[76] for possible prosecution.[77] Flumenbaum, who had graduated *summa cum laude* in History[78] from Columbia University in 1971 and *cum laude* from Harvard Law School in 1974,[79] had recently joined the U.S. Attorney's Office in order to get more trial experience. "It was important for me to feel I could try a long case," he noted in a 1982 interview.[80] Although John Biermans, Assistant Counsel for the Unification Church of America, speculates that Flumenbaum's religious beliefs might have motivated his energetic prosecution,[81] it seems more likely that pure ambition led the young prosecutor to work "eighteen hours a day, seven days a week"[82] on Moon's highly visible case. Flumenbaum wanted to argue the Moon case so badly that when the DOJ had second thoughts about authorizing prosecution, he threatened to quit.[83] Indeed, subsequent events seem to have confirmed the ambition hypothesis; Flumenbaum has since been named partner in the prestigious New York law firm of Paul, Weiss, Rifkind, Wharton & Garrison.[84] As a sidelight on the changing political views of the college students of the early 1970s, it is interesting to note that although under Flumenbaum's editorship[85] the *Columbia Daily Spectator* advertised "JOIN SPEC, [the *Spectator*] FIGHT THE IRS"[86] (the IRS at the time was jeopardizing the newspaper's financial solvency by trying to revoke its tax exempt status),[87] just ten years later he would be fighting *for* the IRS by prosecuting Moon's tax case.

Just after his arraignment in U.S. District Court on October 22, 1981, Rev. Moon spoke to supporters at a rally in New York City's Foley Square. In his speech he openly questioned the prosecution's motives:

> I would not be standing here today if my skin were white or my religion were Presbyterian. I am here today only because my skin is yellow and my religion is Unification Church. The ugliest things in this beautiful country of America are religious bigotry and racism.[88]

Moon followed up this attack by moving on March 10, 1982, for a "bench trial on the ground that pervasive public hostility precluded the selection of a fair and impartial jury."[89]   Indeed, the judge himself admitted that Moon was the object of "substantial unpopularity . . . in the public eye," so much so that the public's hostility might "imperil [Moon's] opportunity of getting a fair jury trial."[90]

A pre-trial opinion survey of possible jury candidates by pollster Stephen Roth revealed strong prejudice against Moon. Of the 1,000 people interviewed,

> 76.4% respond[ed] unfavorably to the name "Reverend Moon," 70.4% unfavorably to the name "Sun Myung Moon," 67.3% unfavorably to the term "Moonies" and almost all using such pejorative terms as "crook," "hoax," "racketeer," who "brainwashes" and "exploits the young" to describe Reverend Moon.[91]

Public hostility was so strong that 42.9% admitted that, given the chance, they would "throw Reverend Sun Myung Moon in jail,"[92] without even hearing the evidence against him.

In a letter to the judge, the prosecutor nevertheless argued against a bench trial, since Moon had publicly questioned "the integrity and motives of this prosecution" both in his speech at Foley Square and in a full-page reprint in the *New York Times*. According to the letter, the judge's position in a bench trial would be "untenable," and public interest dictated that the trial both actually be and appear to be fair. Such "fairness" in both fact and appearance, the prosecutor argued, required a jury trial, the traditional method of ensuring fairness.[93] This argument, however, seems more likely to ensure the appearance of a fair trial if Moon were convicted than to ensure a fair trial in fact, no matter what its outcome. The prosecutor seemed less concerned about whether a jury trial might be more biased than a bench trial than about whether a jury might appear less biased in the event of a conviction.

Despite his "reservations about the ability of even a searching *voir dire* to pick out those who may have what are to them known biases [toward a 'distinctly unpopular' defendant] that they do not chose to reveal,"[94] the judge felt compelled by federal law to deny Moon's request for a bench trial.[95] He thus presided over a marathon *voir dire* of seven days and 80 jury candidates.[96] Since, as the judge admitted, "to the extent people know about [Rev. Moon] and his religion it is true that their attitudes are negative,"[97] the supposedly unbiased jury members eventually selected would "tend to be the less educated and less intelligent people."[98] He also doubted the ability of such a jury to understand a "complicated" case.[99]

As it turned out, Judge Goettel himself seemed to have difficulty understanding the testimony. He later commented that Flumenbaum would "go off in labrynthian details that no one else could follow . . . Marty [Flumenbaum] came up with extremely complicated arguments, almost Talmudic, but if you spent enough time you could follow them out."[100] If a federal judge admitted having problems understanding parts of the case, it seems likely that "less intelligent" jurors were completely overwhelmed by the testimony. It is no wonder the judge remarked that, given the kind of a jury *voir dire* produced, "I would have thought it fairer to have this case tried without a jury."[101]

Not only was the jury hardly composed of the "best and the brightest," this group of Moon's "peers" also seemed at least slightly prejudiced against him. Of the twelve people who actually served on the jury, for example, three had heard that the Unification Church "brainwashes" people, two had heard that the Church was a "cult," and another that the "Moonies" were "taking over New York City."[102]

After hearing over four weeks of testimony and deliberating for close to a week,[103] the ten-woman two-man jury delivered its verdict on May 18, 1982:   guilty as charged.   On July 16, Judge Goettel sentenced Moon to concurrent terms of 18 months in prison for the first four counts, and a fine of $25,000 plus costs.[104]

Moon's lawyers proceeded to appeal the conviction to the Court of Appeals for the Second Circuit. The appeals court heard the case on March 23, 1983.[105] This time, noted constitutional lawyer and Harvard Law School professor Laurence Tribe argued the case[106] instead of Charles Stillman, the chief defense lawyer at the district court level.[107]

One of Tribe's key arguments in his initial brief to the Court of Appeals was that the lower court erred in not examining Moon's claim of selective prosecution based on his unpopular religion; for even though the trial judge himself admitted that the IRS "would have been less likely" to investigate Moon's taxes "if he had been the leader of a less controversial religion,"[108] he refused to grant Moon "discovery and a hearing" on his charges of selective prosecution.[109]

As evidence of selective prosecution, Tribe cited Senator Dole's apparent role in initiating the investigation and prosecution, and also noted that the government might have been trying to "rid the country of an unpopular religious leader" since [the DOJ] returned Moon's indictment while he was abroad.[110] Moon would not have had to return to the U.S. for trial since he was traveling at the time in South Korea, which does not have an extradition agreement with the U.S.[111]

In a 2-1 decision, however, the Court of Appeals upheld the lower court's decision, including its position on selective prosecution. The Court noted that before the trial

Moon's defense counsel had not submitted enough evidence to warrant an investigation into the charges of selective prosecution.[112] It also implied that Moon's later evidence for selective prosecution, such as that submitted by Tribe, amounted to no more than "mere suspicion" and "surmise."[113] After the Supreme Court refused to hear his appeal,[114] Moon had no choice but to serve out his prison sentence. He was thus jailed, one could argue, essentially for his unorthodox religious beliefs and practices.

This apparent attempt by the IRS and DOJ to "get" the leader of a "religious cult" is reminiscent of a similar use of tax prosecution to punish "undesirables": the tax trials of underworld figures in the 1920s and 1930s. According to William Slocum, a student of the revenue service of the period, charging mobsters and others with tax crimes was the only way to prevent the "people of the United States" from "losing their freedom of action to a lot of underworld thugs and politicians":

> The story is that Elmer Irey's Intelligence Unit [in the Department of the Treasury] was literally the last hope of the American people in our running battle with the underworld. It was a battle the citizenry was losing when the Intelligence Unit unlimbered its courage, cunning, and the income-tax statutes to check an enemy within our borders that had us closer to defeat than has any foreign foe. . . . The Intelligence Unit of the Treasury was our last defense against the Capones, Gordons, Pendergasts, and the Huey Longs.[115]

In the several decades of such tax prosecutions, the Department of the Treasury helped in "bringing to justice" such noted criminals as Alphonse Capone,[116] Bruno Richard Hauptmann,[117] Huey Long,[118] William Frad,[119] "Waxie"

Gordon,[120] and Johnny Torrio.[121]   Although few would doubt that any one of these underworld figures was guilty of crimes far more severe than tax evasion, the government apparently found such charges easiest to prove.

Though few government officials would blush at admitting that they were trying to "get" mobsters, they might redden if forced to concede that they were trying to imprison "cult leaders." Yet the deep-seated fear of Moon and widespread revulsion of the supposed religious beliefs and practices of his church apparently persuaded the IRS and the DOJ to investigate and prosecute him, no matter how exceptional or legally indefensible such actions were. That many religious leaders realized the dangerous precedent that *United States v. Moon* was setting and overlooked his unorthodox beliefs enough to defend him seems not to have mattered because their support came too late and because rank-and-file laypersons probably did not agree with their religious leaders' defense of Moon.

Notes

1.   It should be noted in passing that the definition of a "cult" is extremely nebulous and seems to depend as much on the attitude of the speaker as on the actual characteristics of the group being described.

2.   Commissioner of Internal Revenue and the Chief Counsel for the Internal Revenue Service, the U.S. Internal Revenue Service, *Annual Report 1981,* (Washington, D.C.: Government Printing Office, 1982), p. 5.

3.   Ibid., p. 12.

4.   Ibid., pp. 5 & 12.

5.   W. Curtis Elliott, Jr., "CA-9 in *Dalstrom* Analyzes Effect of Tax Law Uncertainty on Criminal Prosecutions," *The Journal of Taxation,* vol. 62, no. 3, March 1985, p. 150.

6.   Colleen S. Yamaguchi, "Uncertainty in the Law: An Uncertain Defense in Criminal Tax Prosecutions," *Tax Lawyer,* vol. 39, no. 2, p. 387; see, for example, *United States v. Mallas,* 762 F.2d 361, 363 (4th Cir. 1985).

7.   Darrell McGowen, et al., *Criminal and Civil Tax Fraud* (New York, NY: Kluwer Law Book Publishers, Inc., 1986), vol. 1, p. x.

8.   Commissioner of Internal Revenue, p. 16.

9.   *United States v. Moon,* 718 F.2d 1210, 1216 (1983).   Moon was convicted of violating 18 U.S.C. § 371, 26 U.S.C. § 7206(1), 18 U.S.C. § 1001, and 18 U.S.C. § 1503.

10.   Data for this calculation came from the Administrative Office of the U.S. Courts' *United States District Courts Sentences Imposed Chart* (Washington, D.C.:   Government Printing Office), for the periods 1977-78, 1978-79, 1979-80, 1980-81, 1981-82, 1982-83, 1983-84, and 1984-86; and *United States v. Moon,* 718 F.2d 1210, 1216 (1983).   From the total population of defendants convicted under 18 U.S.C. § 371, the percentage falling into the *Sentences Imposed Chart*'s "imprisoned" category was calculated.   All those defendants in this category were sorted by length of prison term, length of probation term, and amount of fine, and then compared with Moon's total sentence. From this comparison, Moon's percentile rank among those in the "imprisonment" category was

calculated, and then his rank in the "imprisoned" group was adjusted to make it reflect his rank in relation to the entire population of those sentenced. Most calculations were performed using MINITAB on a VAX mainframe computer.

11.   U.S. Congress, Senate, Committee on the Judiciary, Subcommittee on the Constitution, *Issues in Religious Liberty* (Washington, D.C.: Government Printing Office, 1984), Ninety-Eighth Congress, Second Session, June 26, 1986, Serial No. J-98-124; hereinafter referred to as "Hatch hearing."

12.   Senator Orrin G. Hatch, letter to Edward Bennett Williams, June 11, 1985, p. 2.

13.   Senator Orrin G. Hatch, letter to author, January 5, 1988.

14.   Hatch, letter to Williams, p. 2.

15.   Ibid., pp. 2-3.

16.   Ibid., p. 4.

17.   Hatch, letter to author.

18.   Hatch hearing, p. 180.

19.   Unification Church of America, "Outline of Reverend Moon's Case," information statement (New York, NY: 1984?), p. 15.

20.   718 F.2d 1210, 1216.

21.   718 F.2d 1210, 1216-1217.

22. Larry Tell, "The Reverend Moon's Money," *The National Law Journal,* May 17, 1982, p. 6.

23. Ibid., p. 6.

24. John T. Biermans, *The Odyssey of New Religious Movements; Persecution, Struggle, Legitimation: A Case Study of the Unification Church* (Lewiston, NY: Edwin Mellen Press, 1986), p. 158.

25. Laurence Tribe, "Brief for Appellant Sun Myung Moon," *United States v. Sun Myung Moon and Takeru Kamiyama,* Case No. 82-1275, United States Court of Appeals for the Second Circuit, November 30, 1982, p. 69.

26. Steven McDowell and Thomas Monaghan, "Brief for the Catholic League for Religious and Civil Rights as Amicus Curiae," *Sun Myung Moon, et al., v. United States of America,* Case No. 83-1242, petition for certiorari in the Supreme Court of the United States, October term, 1983, p. 3.

27. Albert Blaustein, "Brief Amicus Curiae of the Freemen Institute in Support of Petition for Certiorari," *Sun Myung Moon, et al., v. United States of America,* Case No. 83-1242, petition for certiorari in the Supreme Court of the United States, October term, 1983, pp. 10-20.

28. Gary Klott, "The Key Issues in PTL Case," *New York Times,* June 16, 1987, p. D2.

29. "3 Federal Agencies Open Criminal Inquiry on PTL Ministry," *New York Times,* June 11, 1987, p. A18.

30. "Grand Jury Opens Inquiry on PTL Ministries' Finances," *New York Times,* August 18, 1987, p. A17.

31. William E. Schmidt, "Justice Dept. Sifting Bakker Finances," *New York Times,* May 29, 1987, p. A16.

32. "Archbishop Protests Arms," *New York Times,* February 14, 1982, p. 42.

33. Bill McAllister, "'Peace Bishop' Known as Publicity-Shy Boat-Rocker," *The Washington Post,* November 12, 1986, p. A3.

34. Unification Church of America, p. 15.

35. Herbert Richardson, ed., *Constitutional Issues in the Case of Reverend Moon: Amicus Briefs Presented to the United States Supreme Court* (Lewiston, NY: Edwin Mellen Press, 1984), Table of Contents.

36. "Coalition in Dallas Seeks Action on Religious Liberty," *New York Tribune,* August 22, 1984, in Committee to Defend the U.S. Constitution, "Who's Next?" reprint of advertisement in *The Washington Post* (Washington, D.C.: 1984?).

37. "Moon's Attorney Predicts 'Historic Battle,'" *The Washington Post,* September 15, 1983, in Committee to Defend.

38. "300 Clergy Protest Rev. Moon Jail Term," (AP), *The Washington Times,* May 31, 1984, in Committee to Defend.

39. Coalition for Religious Freedom Rally, Washington, D.C., May 30, 1984, in Committee to Defend.

40. "Persecuting Rev. Moon," *South Holland-Pointer Economist,* Chicago, IL, May 23, 1985, in Committee to Defend.

41. Paul Cobb, "Moon Victim of Gov't Conspiracy, Senate Committee Review Exposes Facts," *Oakland Post,* July 3, 1985, in Committee to Defend.

42. The Phil Donahue Show, Chicago, IL, May 16, 1984, in Committee to Defend.

43. Richardson, Table of Contents.

44. David E. Anderson, "Moon Case Called Threat to Religious Freedom," *New Jersey Law Journal,* Vol. 112, December 8, 1983, p. 621.

45. Colman McCarthy, "The Real Issue in the Case of Rev. Moon," *The Washington Post,* February 5, 1984, in Biermans, p. 159.

46. "Brief of the Sparticist League as Amicus Curiae," in Richardson, pp. 627-657.

47. Biermans, pp. 173-175.

48. *Sun Myung Moon v. United States, cert. denied,* 466 U.S. 971 (1984).

49. Charles Rice, speaking at the First Annual Conference on Religious Liberty, Washington, D.C., 1984, in Committee to Defend.

50. *U.S. v. Moon,* U.S. District Court for the Southern District of New York, pre-trial hearing transcript (hereinafter referred to as "Pre-Trial Transcript"), pp. 353-359, in Tribe, p. 20.

51. *The Merit Report* (New York, NY: Philip Morris, Inc., 1982), July 29, 1982, question 6.

52. Hollander, Cohen Associates, survey #5000, September 1984, (Baltimore, MD), p. 9, question 46a.

53. "Cults Lead List of Groups 'Not Wanted as Neighbors,'" *The Gallup Report,* January/February 1987, Report No. 256-257 (Princeton, NJ: 1987), pp. 19-20.

54. *Transcript of Proceedings: Information Meeting on the Cult Phenomenon in the United States* (Washington, D.C.: Ace Federal Reporters, Inc., 1979), February 5, 1979, p. 21.

55. Edward F. Canfield, "Brief Amici Curiae for Bishop Ernest L. Unterkoefler, Clare Boothe Luce, Eugene J. McCarthy, Robert Destro and a Coalition of Catholic Laymen," *Moon v. United States,* Case No. 83-1242, petition for *certiorari* in the Supreme Court of the United States, October term, 1983, p. 1a.

56. Ibid., p. 1a.

57. Ibid., p. 2a.

58. Ibid., pp. 1a-2a.

59. Ibid., p. 3a.

60. Charles Brownson, *Congressional Staff Directory, 1976* (Mount Vernon, VA: Congressional Staff Directory, 1976), 18th ed., p. 196.

61. Michael Barone et al., *The Almanac of American Politics, 1978* (New York, NY: E.P. Dutton, 1977), p. 299.

62. Charles Brownson, *Congressional Staff Directory, 1981* (Mount Vernon, VA: Congressional Staff Directory, 1981), pp. 188-189.

63. *Bob Jones University v. United States,* 103 S. Ct. 2017 (1983).

64. *Transcript of Proceedings,* p. 21.

65. Ibid., cover.

66. Ibid., pp. 34, 68, 72 & 77-78.

67. Ibid., pp. 123, 125-126.

68. Ibid., p. 122.

69. Ibid., p. 123.

70. Robert Z. Alpern, et al., letter of January 30, 1979, to Senator Robert Dole, in Ibid., pp. 160-161.

71. *Transcript of Proceedings,* pp. 50-51.

72. Ibid., p. 46.

73. Ibid., p. 51.

74. Ibid., p. 39.

75. Ibid., p. 51.

76. *Martindale-Hubbell Law Directory, 1988* (New Providence, NJ: Martindale Hubbell, Inc., 1988), 120th ed., vol. V, p. 1167B.

77. Alissa Rubin, "Bulldog Prosecutor Returns to Paul, Weiss," *The American Lawyer,* November 1982, p. 101.

78. Ibid., p. 101.

79. *Martindale-Hubbell,* p. 1167B.

80. Rubin, p. 101.

81. John T. Biermans, Assistant Counsel for the Unification Church of America, interview by telephone with author, October 22, 1987.

82. Rubin, p. 101.

83. Ibid., p. 101.

84. *Martindale-Hubbell,* p. 1167B.

85. *Columbia Daily Spectator,* masthead, September 16, 1970, p. 8.

86. *Columbia Daily Spectator,* advertisement, October 21, 1970, p. 2.

87. "IRS Investigates *Spectator;* Tax Exemption Threatened," *Columbia Daily Spectator,* September 16, 1970, p. 1.

88. 718 F.2d 1210, 1217.

89. Pre-Trial Transcript, p. 330, in Tribe, p. 4.

90. Ibid., pp. 372 & 381, in Tribe, p. 20.

91. *U.S. v. Moon,* U.S. District Court for the Southern District of New York, joint appendix (hereinafter

referred to as "Joint Appendix"), pp. 801-803, 822 & 916-1002, in Tribe, p. 20.

92.   Joint Appendix, pp. 819-820, in Tribe, p. 20.

93.   718 F.2d 1210, 1217.

94.   Pre-Trial Transcript, p. 381, in Tribe, pp. 20-21.

95.   Tribe, pp. 19-20.

96.   *U.S. v. Moon*, U.S. District Court for the Southern District of New York, trial transcript (hereinafter referred to as "Trial Transcript"), in Tribe, p. 21.

97.   Trial Transcript, p. 1758, in Tribe, p. 22.

98.   Ibid., pp. 1759-1760, in Tribe, p. 24.

99.   Ibid., p. 1760, in Tribe, p. 24.

100. Rubin, p. 101.

101. Trial Transcript, p. 1760, in Tribe, p. 24.

102. Ibid., pp. 473, 857, 1394, 1514-1515, 2052 & 2106, in Tribe, p. 23.

103. Unification Church of America, p. 15.

104. 718 F.2d 1210, 1216.

105. 718 F.2d 1210.

106. Tribe, cover.

107. Tell, p. 6.

108. *U.S. v. Moon,* United States District Court for the Southern District of New York, post-trial hearing transcript (hereinafter referred to as "Post-Trial Transcript"), pp. 36-37, in Tribe, p. 67.

109. Pre-Trial Transcript, p. 166; and Post-Trial Transcript, p. 92, in Tribe, p. 67.

110. Post-Trial Transcript, p. 162, in Tribe, p. 68.

111. Igor I. Kovass and Adolf Sprudzs, *Current Treaty Index 1984* (Buffalo, NY: William S. Hein, & Co., Inc., 1984) 3rd ed., pp. 313-314.

112. 718 F.2d 1210, 1229.

113. 718 F.2d 1210, 1230.

114. 466 U.S. 971.

115. Elmer L. Irey and William Slocum, *The Tax Dodgers: The Inside Story of the T-Men's War with America's Political and Underworld Hoodlums* (New York, NY: Greenberg Publisher, 1948), pp. viii & ix; see also Alan Hynd, *The Giant Killers* (New York, NY: Robert McBride & Co., 1945).

116. Irey, p. 56.

117. Ibid., pp. 66-87.

118. Ibid., pp. 88-117.

119. Ibid., pp. 121-123.

120. Ibid., pp. 134-153.

121. Ibid., pp. 154-165.

Chapter IV

The Abortion-Clinic Bombers

This last case of the abortion-clinic bombers shows how the government deals with those lawbreakers whose religiously inspired acts Americans view as "dangerous" or "extreme," even if these offenders' religious beliefs and practices are "moderate." Although the controversy over abortion continues to inflame policy-makers and the public, only a few extremists are willing to carry their opposition to abortion so far as to firebomb abortion clinics. Confronted with such violent means of protest, most Americans have overwhelmingly condemned the bombers. Only a few of the most militant "Pro-Lifers" fail to object to the bombers' actions.

In general, the government has reacted vigorously and effectively against the bombers. The Bureau of Alcohol, Tobacco and Firearms made the abortion cases its top priority and unleashed almost one half of its resources to solve them even though the abortion bombings make up only a tiny fraction of all such crimes. BATF has solved many more abortion-related firebombings than those not inspired by anti-abortion sentiments, and the Department of Justice has ensured that those abortion-clinic bombers apprehended receive stiff sentences for their crimes.

* * * * * *

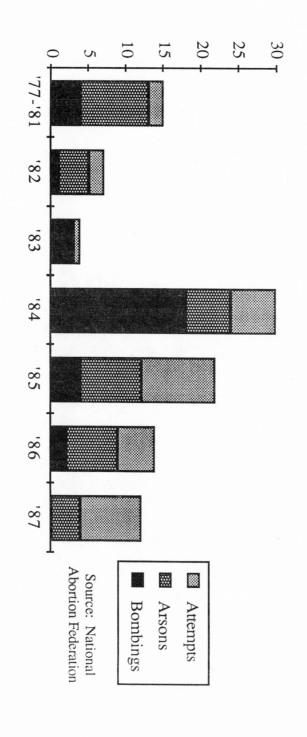

Chart IV-1
Incidents of Reported Bombings, Arsons, and Attempts

Attempts

Arsons

Bombings

Source: National
Abortion Federation

As crimes go, bombings are especially terrifying. Or as Stephen Higgins, the Director of the Bureau of Alcohol, Tobacco and Firearms (BATF), puts it:

Few crimes are more reprehensible in the view of the American public than criminal bombings. By their very nature, bombings pose an indiscriminate threat to each of us. These crimes strike at the very heart of a free society, promoting fear and anxiety among the citizens of this nation.[1]

Thus, only the most ardent anarchists would object to punishing such violent acts. Indeed, the U.S. Code contains several sections punishing bombings. One under which many prosecutions are brought is 18 U.S.C. § 844(i):

Whoever maliciously damages or destroys, or attempts to damage or destroy, by means of fire or an explosive, any building, vehicle, or other real or personal property used in interstate or foreign commerce or in any activity affecting interstate or foreign commerce shall be imprisoned for not more than ten years or fined not more than $10,000, or both; and if personal injury results shall be imprisoned for not more than twenty years or fined not more than $20,000, or both; and if death results shall also be subject to imprisonment for any term of years, or to the death penalty or to life imprisonment as provided in section 34 of this title.

Thanks to BATF and DOJ, this section is more than just empty words. Between June 30, 1984, and June 30, 1986, the Department of Justice obtained convictions for 72 violations of 18 U.S.C. § 844(i).[2]

Since the Supreme Court handed down *Roe v. Wade,*[3] the controversial 1973 decision which legalized most abortions, opponents have used various methods of protesting the Court's policy, including writing letters, lobbying,[4] holding marches,[5] picketing,[6] and even sit-ins and non-violent civil disobedience at abortion clinics.[7] Yet relatively few "Pro-Lifers" have ever used violence in their efforts to stop abortion. In the past few years, however, a handful of opponents of *Roe v. Wade* have targeted abortion clinics for arson or firebombing (see Chart IV-1). From 1982 to 1987, for example, the National Abortion Federation received reports of 29 arsons, 28 bombings, and 32 attempted arsons or bombings, all of which were directed at abortion providers.[8] Although even most opponents of abortion agree that the government should somehow punish these bombers and arsonists, it seems the Bureau of Alcohol, Tobacco and Firearms and the Department of Justice have investigated and prosecuted these cases more zealously than those bombings and arsons that were not motivated by anti-abortion sentiments.

Apparently in reaction to substantial public pressure, which will be discussed in greater detail below, the Reagan Administration urged the Department of Justice and other appropriate federal agencies to make investigation and prosecution of the bombers a priority. On January 3, 1985, the President issued the following press statement:

During the past few months, there has been a series of bombings at abortion clinics throughout the country. I condemn, in the strongest terms, those individuals who perpetrate these and *all such violent, anarchistic activities.* As president of the United States, I will *do all in my power* to assure that the guilty are brought to justice. Therefore, I will request the

Attorney General to see *that all federal agencies with jurisdiction pursue the investigation vigorously.*[9] [Emphasis added.]

Perhaps in response to Reagan's views, that same day then Attorney General William French Smith released his own statement, in which he further specified the agencies involved:

> I join with the President in condemning, in the strongest terms, those individuals who perpetrate the series of bombings at abortion clinics throughout the country.
>
> I have asked FBI Director William H. Webster to take steps to insure that the FBI is providing *all possible assistance* in the investigation of acts of violence against abortion clinics.
>
> In developing these cases, the Bureau of Alcohol, Tobacco and Firearms (BATF), as the lead investigative agency, reports directly to Department of Justice prosecutors on the results of its investigations. Since May of 1982, BATF agents have conducted 30 investigations of bombings of abortion or abortion-related facilities and to date 12 of these investigations have been closed with the arrest of eight persons.
>
> Five persons have been convicted and sentenced to serve in prison in excess of 20 years. In addition, four defendants awaiting trial face sentences in excess of 30 years, if convicted.
>
> Assistance by the FBI in these investigations to date have [sic] included the use of psychological profiling of suspects by the FBI's behavioral science

experts at Quantico, fingerprint checks and criminal record checks of suspects.

The Department of Justice, continuing its intensive work with the Department of Treasury, will continue to investigate, identify, prosecute, and convict those who commit these unlawful acts, to the end that this senseless destruction be stopped.[10] [Emphasis added.]

The BATF, with assistance from the FBI, was thus to investigate these bombings, and the DOJ was to prosecute the suspected perpetrators.

The Bureau of Alcohol, Tobacco and Firearms, for its part, soon made the bombings of abortion clinics a high priority, if not its highest priority. Although BATF Director Stephen Higgins stated at a congressional hearing on "Abortion Clinic Violence" that all "bombings and arsons" are "our No. 1 priority,"[11] in a letter to Representative Don Edwards of December 11, 1985, he later seemed to have limited BATF's area of highest priority to bombings and arsons only of abortion clinics. "The investigation of abortion clinic bombings/arsons," he wrote, "remains ATF's number one priority."[12] In its investigation of these cases, then, BATF appears to have given them a higher priority than comparable, non-abortion-related arsons and bombings.

The number of arsons and bombings that BATF has chosen to emphasize is, compared to the total number of all such crimes reported, quite small. The National Abortion Federation (NAF) reported 92 incidents of attempted or actual arson or bombing of abortion providers during 1977-86.[13] According to BATF's statistics for the same period, the United States witnessed 12,947 arsons, bombings, and attempts.[14] BATF has thus chosen to make its "No. 1

priority" only 0.7% of all reported bombings, arsons, and attempts.   It therefore claims to have given the abortion bombings a higher priority than even those bombings which killed 310 people during this same period.[15] (To date, no one has died in an abortion-clinic bombing,[16] although some bystanders have suffered injuries from "flying glass and debris."[17]) If we look at only the period 1982-86, when the number of bombings of abortion clinics was especially high, similar statistics emerge.   The NAF reported 77 incidents directed at abortion providers,[18] compared to the 5164 incidents BATF noted against all targets.[19] Figures for the period 1982-86, therefore, show that BATF still emphasized only 1.5% of all its cases of arson and bombing. From these very small percentages of abortion-related crimes, it seems that BATF, by making the abortion cases its chief priority, has been extremely selective, especially considering that the agency threw "fully 500 of its 1200 agents at the abortion-clinic incidents."[20]   In the Malvasi case alone, "[t]hree hundred federal agents and [New York City] detectives . . . work[ed] around the clock for weeks" searching for clues.[21]

As further evidence that the abortion bombers have received harsher treatment than comparable offenders, BATF spokespersons assert that the rate of solved to unsolved cases is much higher for the abortion bombings and arsons than for other bombings and arsons. According to Tom Lambert, an official at BATF's investigation division in charge of the investigations of the abortion-clinic bombings, the "clearance" or solved rate for "ordinary" bombings is "much, much lower" than that for the abortion-clinic bombings. Of the 64 abortion cases BATF has investigated since 1982, 40 had been solved as of October of 1987.[22] Lambert's figures would therefore give the abortion bombings a solved rate of 62.5%, which seems fairly high, especially considering that these cases are often very difficult to solve due to the destruction of much or all of the evidence in the act of bombing.[23] Some incidents will probably never be solved because of a total lack of evidence, witnesses, and apparent *modus operandi*.[24] BATF Director Stephen Higgins reported to a congressional subcommittee in March of 1985 that 22 of the 32 anti-abortion incidents his agency had investigated since 1982 had "been closed by conviction or by arrest,"[25] giving an even higher solved rate of 68.8%.

Both abortion advocates and opponents agree that BATF and DOJ have vigorously investigated and prosecuted the abortion cases.   For example, the National Abortion Federation's President, Barbara Radford, was "very satisfied with the investigations of the bombings and the arsons."[26] On the "Pro-Life" side, one of the defense attorneys for the four defendants in Pensacola, Florida, Patrick Monaghan, believes the "ATF is proud of [its] record" on the abortion cases, and notes that its "success rate has been very good."[27] And Charles Rice, professor at Notre Dame Law School and a defense attorney in the trials in Pensacola, Florida, and Everett, Washington, has the impression that the DOJ is being "very severe" with the abortion bombers.[28]

Indeed, if one uses the sentences they received to measure how severely the DOJ has prosecuted them, the abortion bombers as a group appear to have received sentences at least as heavy as if not heavier than other violators convicted of the same federal statutes. For while the mean prison sentence for the total population of those convicted under 18 U.S.C. § 844(i) from 1977-86 was 68.9 months, that for the abortion-clinic bombers was 73.8 months. Although such a difference is not statistically significant ($F=0.03$), it does indicate that the abortion bombers received sentences of at least average severity.[29]

*   *   *   *   *   *

It appears as if at least one of the major causes for the government's apparent severity towards the abortion-clinic bombers is their religious motivation. One might object, of course, that the abortion bombers' religious motivations were irrelevant because the bombers would be blowing up buildings or committing other crimes even if they were not religious. For a few of the anti-abortion defendants, this objection may be valid. Dennis John Malvasi, sentenced in September of 1987 to seven years in prison,[30] had previously been convicted of two crimes, once for a stabbing and the second time for carrying a "loaded, .25 caliber pistol." At the time of his arrest for the bombings of several abortion clinics in New York City, he was in hiding to avoid a warrant from a Florida court on indictments for six weapons felonies.[31] Another convicted bomber, Don "Benny" Anderson,[32] had once fled Texas to avoid sentencing on a "real estate fraud" conviction.[33] This relatively minor, non-violent crime, however, can hardly be compared with Anderson's later violent kidnapings and firebombings, all motivated by his belief that he, as a Mormon, had been chosen by God to stop abortion.[34]

But many, if not most, of those convicted had no previous criminal records and probably never would have committed any crimes if their religious convictions had not persuaded them to firebomb abortion clinics. Eighteen-year-old Kaye Wiggins, for example, said she helped blow up several abortion clinics in Pensacola, Florida, on Christmas Day, 1984, as "a gift to Jesus on his birthday." Wiggins was also aided by another eighteen-year-old woman, Kathy Simmons.[35] Neither had had a criminal record,[36] and neither fit the stereotype of the fanatical religious terrorist. Friends described Curtis Beseda, sentenced to 20 years in prison for bombings in Everett, Washington,[37] as "law-abiding, gentle and shy." Strongly motivated by his religious convictions, he had worked as a school teacher before firebombing the clinics.[38] Tom Hillier, his lawyer, said Beseda was "as honest and sincere and selfless as any client I have ever represented."[39] At least some of the bombers would probably not have been committing felonies if it had not been for their religious conviction that abortion is immoral.

Regardless of whether they would have become criminals had they not opposed abortion, the abortion-clinic bombers could not escape the label of "religious fanatics." In a hearing on "Abortion Clinic Violence," abortion activist Bill Baird lashed out at the bombers:

> For someone to blow up clinics on Christmas Day, saying they [sic] are doing it 'as a birthday present for the baby Jesus' is unconscionable. Much terrorism has taken place at the hands of those who say God has told them to perform these acts. . . . People arriving at my Suffolk County, Long Island center on Saturdays are often confronted by religious fanatics jumping up and down and speaking in 'tongues.' . . . I am afraid that unless the proper authorities intervene, this nation will turn into another Iran, a country torn apart by religious zealots.[40]

Another doctor whose clinic had been firebombed noted that "Sane people you don't worry about, but religious fanatics you have to worry about."[41]

Considering the criticism that the abortion bombers received from both "Pro-Choice" and "Pro-Life" groups, and only the slightest toleration or feeble support from the opponents of abortion, it is hardly surprising that the government treated them severely. Advocates of legalized abortion, the targets of the bombings and arsons, obviously opposed the attacks vehemently and lobbied the federal government to investigate and prosecute the perpetrators. Patricia Donovan, a writer for Planned Parenthood's *Family Planning Perspectives,* portrayed the bombers as wild-eyed loonies, writing that "by night, inflamed zealots are using bombs, torches and sledgehammers to bring their holy war against abortion to the facilities where abortion is performed."[42] The Director of the Boulder (Colorado) Abortion Clinic, Dr. Warren Hern, characterized the bombings as terrorism and lambasted the Reagan Administration for not vigorously investigating them.[43] And right after the bombings in Pensacola and Washington, D.C., Judy Goldsmith, President of the National Organization for Women, sent a telegram to President Reagan strongly recommending that he condemn "the terrorist acts [of bombing the clinics] in the same strong terms you condemn the attacks of international terrorists upon American citizens."[44] Public opinion seemed to agree; one poll by the Harris organization indicated that 77% of those questioned considered the bombings a "campaign of terrorism."[45]

Although with perhaps less venom, most opponents of abortion also condemned the bombings. Rev. Jerry Falwell, founder of the Moral Majority, commented that the bombers are "not only terrorists, they're criminals."[46] Similarly, Dr. John Wilke, President of the National Right to Life Committee, "abhorred" the "violence," but noted that "the way to stop the violence outside [of the clinics] is to stop the violence inside."[47]

Criticism of the bombings even seeped into the American Christian community's contemporary music, where anti-abortion songs by rock groups are almost

ubiquitous.[48]   Singer and songwriter Steve Taylor, for
example, lambasted the bombers in his 1987 cut "I Blew Up
the Clinic Real Good," and even discounted their motives
and questioned their mental health.[49] Thus, even parts of
the religious "Pro-Life Movement," of which Taylor is
definitely a part,[50] condemn the bombings.

A few "Pro-Lifers," however, only mildly chide or
wholly fail to criticize the bombers. In an op-ed piece
entitled "Bombing Abortion Clinics: It's Violent, But Why
Not?" the Moral Majority's Cal Thomas wrote that
"tactically, as well as politically, the bombing of abortion
clinics is probably not a good idea" but that he "respects the
right of people to do it."[51] On a similar note, activist
Joseph Scheidler has "yet to shed [his] first tear when [he]
sees a charred abortion clinic," and told fellow "Pro-
Lifers," that "we would all rejoice if tomorrow morning we
picked up our newspapers and read that every butchery
mill, every abortion clinic in the United States were burnt
to the bottom."[52]

Apparently in reaction to massive political pressure,
then, DOJ and BATF tried to quash the abortion-clinic
bombers more severely than any other group of bombers.
Against such "religious fanatics" the government spared few
of its prosecutorial weapons. No holds were barred in this
effort to repress these "extreme" actions, even if they were
motivated by the bombers' generally "moderate" religious
beliefs. For it is not their religious beliefs as such that the
public objects to, but rather the extreme actions the
bombers' religious beliefs inspired.

Notes

1. U.S. Bureau of Alcohol, Tobacco and Firearms, *Explosive Incidents Report 1986* (Washington, D.C.: Department of the Treasury, 1987), p. ii.

2. Administrative Office of the U.S. Courts, Statistical Analysis and Reports Division, *United States District Courts Sentences Imposed Chart, Twenty-Four Month Period Ended June 30, 1986* (Washington, D.C.: Government Printing Office, 1987), p. 154.

3. *Roe v. Wade,* 410 U.S. 113 (1973).

4. See, for example, John Wilke's National Right to Life Committee, as described in Patricia Donovan, "The Holy War," *Family Planning Perspectives,* vol. 17, no. 1, January/February 1985, pp. 6-8.

5. George Skelton and Zack Nauth, "President Denounces Abortions, Bombings: Backs Amendment to Protect Unborn, Delivers Pep Talk to 70,000 on Anniversary of Decision," *Los Angeles Times,* January 23, 1985, p. 1.

6. Joseph M. Scheidler, *Closed: 99 Ways to Stop Abortion* (Westchester, IL: Crossway Books, 1985), p. 28.

7. Ibid., p. 131; and Charles Colson, "The Fear of Doing Nothing," *Christianity Today,* vol. 31, May 15, 1987, p. 72.

8. National Abortion Federation, "Incidents of Reported Violence Toward Abortion Providers," computer printout, (Washington, D.C., 1988).

9. U.S. Congress, House of Representatives, Committee on the Judiciary, Subcommittee on Civil and Constitutional Rights, *Abortion Clinic Violence* (Washington, D.C.: Government Printing Office, 1987), March 6, 12, and April 3, 1985; and December 17, 1986, Ninety-Ninth Congress, First and Second Sessions, Serial No. 115, p. 624.

10. Ibid., pp. 625-626.

11. Ibid., p. 92.

12. Ibid., p. 632.

13. National Abortion Federation, "Incidents. . . ."

14. U.S. Bureau of Alcohol, Tobacco and Firearms, p. 11.

15. Ibid., p. 15.

16. National Abortion Federation, "The Threat to Health Care Workers and Patients: Antiabortion Violence and Harassment," information bulletin (Washington, D.C.: January, 1988).

17. U.S. Bureau of Alcohol, Tobacco and Firearms, p. 43.

18. National Abortion Federation, "Incidents. . . ."

19. U.S. Bureau of Alcohol, Tobacco and Firearms, p. 11.

20. Ed Magnuson, "Explosions Over Abortion: More Clinic Bombings Spur Widespread Concern and Controversy," *Time,* vol. 125, January 14, 1985, p. 16.

21. Samuel G. Freedman, "Portrait of an Extremist: Suspect in N.Y. Abortion-Clinic Bombings, Nation's Most Serious Attacks Provide Glimpse of a Movement's Most Radical Elements," *Los Angeles Daily Journal,* vol. 100, May 21, 1987, p. 22.

22. Tom Lambert, Investigative Division, Bureau of Alcohol, Tobacco and Firearms, interview by telephone with author, October 16, 1987.

23. Ibid.

24. Patrick Monaghan, Free Speech Advocates, interview by telephone with author, October 26, 1987.

25. U.S. Congress, p. 79.

26. Rita Ciolli, "Now There's Praise for U.S. Probes," *Newsday,* January 20, 1985, in NewsBank microfiche HEA 1:A14 (1985).

27. Monaghan.

28. Professor Charles Rice, Notre Dame Law School, interview by telephone with author, October 22, 1987.

29. Data for these calculations came from the clerks of the court for the U.S. District Courts in which the bombers were sentenced, and from the *Sentences Imposed Chart* (cited above) for the periods 1977-78, 1978-79, 1979-80, 1980-81, 1981-82, 1982-83, 1983-84, and 1984-86. The amount of prison time, probation time, and/or fine that each defendant received was entered as one row of data in the MINITAB statistics program on a VAX mainframe computer. Where a felon received no prison time,

the amount of time entered in the "prison" column was 0, and a similar procedure was followed for the "probation" and "fine" columns. The "prison" columns were then compared using the "AOVONEWAY" command in MINITAB to calculate the means and 95% confidence intervals for both the total population and abortion bombers, as well as to figure "F" for the ANOVA test of similarity between two populations.

30. U.S. District Court for the Southern District of New York, "Judgment and Probation/Commitment Order" for Dennis John Malvasi, Case No. Cr. 00176-01 (TPG), New York, NY, September 2, 1987.

31. Freedman, p. 22.

32. U.S. District Court for the Eastern Division of Virginia, docket sheet for Don Benny Anderson, Case No. 83-00159-01, Alexandria, VA, 1983.

33. Charles Bosworth Jr. and Girard C. Steichen, "Recruits in the 'Army of God,'" *St. Louis* [MO] *Post-Dispatch,* August 12, 1984, in NewsBank microfiche, HEA 78:A11 (1984).

34. Ibid.

35. Magnuson, pp. 16-17.

36. Andrea Rowand, "Two Women are Charged in Bombings," (Jacksonville) *Florida Times-Union,* January 3, 1985, in NewsBank microfiche, HEA 1:C5 (1985).

37. U.S. District Court for the Western District of Washington, "Judgment and Commitment Order," Case No. CR84-222M (C), Seattle, WA, December 28, 1984.

38.   Jim Haley, "Terrorist? Martyr? No, Says Arsonist: His Only Object was to 'Do What's Right,'" *The* (Everett, WA) *Herald,* December 19, 1984, 2nd edition, p. 1.

39.   Jim Haley, "Abortion Arsonist to Focus Appeal on What He Sees as Greater Evil," *The* (Everett, WA) *Herald,* December 21, 1984, 2nd edition, p. 3A.

40.   U.S. Congress, pp. 576-578.

41.   Mark Travis, "Abortion Clinic Bombers Enter Federal Prison," *Saint Petersburg* [FL] *Times,* June 18, 1985, in NewsBank microfiche HEA 59:B1 (1985).

42.   Donovan, p. 5.

43.   Warren M. Hern, "With Reagan's Blessing, It's Open Season on Abortion Clinics," *Los Angeles Daily Journal,* vol. 97, December 31, 1984, p. 4.

44.   Magnuson, p. 16.

45.   Louis Harris, "Americans Abhor Attacks on Abortion Clinics," *The Harris Survey,* 1985, #10, February 5, 1985, p. 2.

46.   Nancy Keebler, "Bombings Anger Area Abortion Activists," *Sacramento* (CA) *Bee,* January 3, 1985, in NewsBank microfiche HEA 1:B4 (1985).

47.   Donovan, p. 9.

48.   See, for example, Degarmo & Key, "It's A Shame," in *Communication,* record (Nashville, TN: Power Discs, The Benson Co., Inc., 1984); Resurrection Band, "The Chair" and "Little Children," in *Mommy*

Doesn't Love Daddy Anymore, record (Waco, TX: Light Records, Lexicon Music, Inc., 1981); Steve Taylor, "Baby Doe," in *Meltdown,* record (Canoga Park, CA: Sparrow Records, 1983); Steve Camp, "Bad News for Modern Man," in *Shake Me to Wake Me,* audiotape (Canoga Park, CA: Sparrow Records, 1985); and Phil Keaggy, "The Little Ones," *Ph'lipside,* audiotape, (Canoga Park, CA: Sparrow Records, 1982).

49.   Steve Taylor, "I Blew Up the Clinic Real Good," *I Predict 1990,* audiotape (Waco, TX: Myrrh Records, 1987).

50.   See, for example, Taylor, "Baby Doe."

51.   Cal Thomas, "Bombing Abortion Clinics: It's Violent, But Why Not?" *Los Angeles Times,* November 27, 1984, part II, p. 5.

52.   Donovan, p. 7.

Chapter V

Implications

As these three cases have illustrated, the government's official protestations of strict neutrality toward religion sometimes seem suspect at best. If the government did adjust its treatment of religiously inspired offenders according to their religion, the Sanctuary Movement won in this arrangement, and the Rev. Moon and the abortion-clinic bombers lost. The government overlooked the Sanctuary Movement's "humanitarian" law breaking, but tried to stamp out violations by "cult leaders" like Moon and "dangerous religious fanatics" like the abortion bombers. In none of these three cases can the government claim complete victory for the forces of "law and order." The Sanctuary Movement continues to smuggle and shelter undocumented Central Americans and to expand more than its founders ever dreamed possible. The Unification Church, still headed by Rev. Moon, continues to proselytize American youth and increase its financial holdings in the U.S., and Unificationists like John Biermans believe that Moon actually rose in the public's eyes by being thrown in prison for the cause of "religious liberty."[1] Although the number of abortion-clinic bombings has decreased since BATF made them its top priority, they have by no means stopped, and it remains unwise to be in the vicinity of an American abortion clinic after dark.

Perhaps this lack of total success brings into question the myth of the "invincible federal government." If the government cannot stop priests and nuns from disobeying its immigration laws or religious maniacs like Anderson from kidnapping abortion doctors and burning down their clinics, perhaps we should expect more ambiguous results in other areas of law enforcement. Agencies like the Department of Justice may be able to temper or reduce disobedience of the law, but they cannot prevent all violations. At best they can punish offenders after the fact and hope that those contemplating similar crimes will be dissuaded by their example. Punishment of all criminals will not necessarily lead to the end of all crime.

But whatever the federal government's success in preventing law breaking, these cases do seem to show that public pressure persuaded government officials to alter their normal behavior towards religiously inspired offenders. The government treated none of the three groups in this study as would be expected; that is, the government did not treat the groups strictly according to the severity of their violations, but more according to their religious motivations. None of the religiously motivated offenders received treatment comparable to that received by secularly motivated violators of the the same federal statutes. No one could have accurately predicted how the government would deal with the religious groups by looking at the severity of their violations alone. Their religious motivations and the public's opinion of those motivations had to be considered as well.

Another point worth mentioning is the paradox that under a conservative Republican administration, left-leaning groups such as the Sanctuary Movement have fared better than right-leaning groups like the Unification Church and the abortion-clinic bombers. The government would therefore seem to respond to public pressure regardless of the policies of a particular administration. For without strong public pressure in favor of harsh measures, the Reagan Administration might not have investigated or prosecuted Moon, an outspoken patriot and anti-Communist who seeks to strengthen "traditional family values." Absent the public's vehement opposition, the Reagan Administration might have prosecuted the abortion-clinic bombers less zealously than it did since Reagan does agree with the bombers' goal, the criminalization of abortion, if perhaps not with their violent means. Finally, the Reagan Administration undoubtedly would have loved to quash its political enemies in the Sanctuary Movement, but public pressure restrained it.

Another way of interpreting these cases would be to consider how these three groups seem to tolerate religions different from their own. Evidence from the three cases just examined would seem to confirm the hypothesis that, in a liberal society, those whom the public perceives as tolerant will be tolerated, but those it perceives as intolerant will not be.

In this study, Rev. Moon and the abortion-clinic bombers would illustrate the fate of the supposedly intolerant. Both have the reputation of espousing an "only us" philosophy of intolerance, exclusion, or "election" in the Calvinist sense of the word, and for the most part the government has treated them harshly, or not "tolerated" them. The Sanctuary Movement, on the other hand, gives the impression of tolerating a wide range of religious persuasions, and the government has dealt with them leniently, or "tolerated" them.

For the cases studied, then, my research would suggest the pattern shown in Table V-1. By putting pressure on the federal law enforcement agencies, the public might be seen as indirectly "punishing" religious intolerance and "rewarding" religious toleration in these three cases.

Table V-1
The Relationship Between the Public's Perception of a Group's Toleration and the Government's Treatment of Group

	Public's perception of group's toleration:	Federal government's treatment of group:
Sanctuary Movement	tolerant	lenient
Reverend Moon	intolerant	severe
Abortion-Clinic Bombers	intolerant	severe

In religion the Sanctuary Movement tries to portray itself as tolerant, moderate, and "reasonable." Religiously, their membership is more than ecumenical, including Roman Catholics, Baptists, United Christians, Quakers, Unitarians, Presbyterians, Methodists, Episcopalians, Lutherans, Brethren, Universalists, Mennonites, Christian Disciples, Jews,[2] and even "unbelievers."[3] Furthermore, the Movement's leaders never cease to recruit new participants by holding press conferences,[4] issuing pastoral letters,[5] and publishing "how-to" guides.[6] The Movement's organizers hardly want to limit participation to only the "doctrinally correct." Perhaps in response, the government has pampered them.

Despite the Unification Church's ecumenical conferences[7] and name ("The Holy Spirit Association for the Unification of World Christianity"[8]), the public seems to view it as monolithic and intolerant. Perhaps the Church's theology has caused much of this impression. Unificationists look upon Rev. Moon as a modern-day

"prophet"[9] or "messenger from God."[10] Some students of
the Church claim that members sometimes address him as
"Father," and even suggest that he believes himself to be a
kind of Messiah.[11] Although the Church goes out of its way
to recruit new members,[12] such efforts often tend to
reinforce the public's negative image of the Church, as
recent cases involving "deprogramming" testify.[13]

If any one of the three groups studied deserves to be
called intolerant, it has to be the abortion-clinic bombers.
Their zeal and claims of direction from God send chills
down the spine of "Pro-Choice" activists. Don Benny
Anderson, later convicted of blowing up several abortion
clinics[14] and kidnapping a doctor who performed abortions,
claimed he was on a "mission . . . commanded by God" to
fight abortion.[15] In a ransom letter he issued just after
kidnapping the doctor and his wife, he claimed to be God,
Jesus Christ, the Archangel Gabriel, and a member of the
"Army of God." His "Decree of God" opens, "I, God, direct
this epistle to my son, President Reagan, and all the
inhabitants of this land," and ends, "I, Gabriel, have
requested the annihilation of your [Reagan's] soul and the
eradication of this degenerate nation before the council of
the Father's [sic]."[16] Although Anderson might be more
extreme than the other bombers, the bombers as a group
certainly could not be called very tolerant of points of view
other than their own.

It is hardly surprising that advocates of the current
abortion policy, like Bill Baird, branded the bombers
"religious fanatics":[17]

Rather than expressing a tolerance for the religious
beliefs of others. [sic] many of these "religious"
organizations are encouraging lawlessness and
destruction in the name of God. Rather than use their

positions in a responsible way to encourage more reasonable doctrine, many clergy are guilty of turning loose emotionally disturbed people to inflict pain, injury and damage to others. . . . I am afraid that unless the proper authorities intervene, this nation will turn into another Iran, a country *torn apart by religious zealots* with total disregard for the rights of others.[18] [Emphasis added.]

On a similar note, Dr. William Permenter, whose office in Pensacola, Florida, was firebombed, commented, "Sane people you don't worry about, but religious fanatics you have to worry about."[19]

A group's perceived tolerance of other religions or religious manifestations then, seems to correlate positively with the government's "tolerance" of their supposed or actual law breaking. It seems that the tolerant are tolerated, but those who appear intolerant are not tolerated.

It can certainly be argued that such "discrimination" on the basis of a group's degree of religious tolerance violates the principle of strict governmental neutrality toward religion. A contradiction would therefore seem to exist between the supposed principles of Liberalism and the actual practices of a "Liberal" government like that of the United States. But perhaps we would do well to examine Liberalism as championed by its founders instead of trying to use our nebulous, twentieth-century American version of "true Liberalism." Even John Locke, as worthy as any of the title of "Founder of Liberalism," did not advocate such extreme governmental "neutrality" toward religion as some of today's strict civil libertarians would have us believe. In his *Letter Concerning Toleration,* for example, Locke argues that the government should distinguish between the religiously tolerant and the religiously intolerant:

Nobody, therefore, in fine, neither single persons nor churches, nay, nor even commonwealths, have any just title to invade the civil rights and worldly goods of each other upon pretence of religion. . . .

But to come to particulars. I say, first, no opinions contrary to human society or to those moral rules which are necessary to the preservation of civil society, are to be tolerated by the magistrate. . . .

Another more secret evil, but more dangerous to the commonwealth, is when men arrogate to themselves, and to those of their own sect, some peculiar prerogative covered over with a specious show of deceitful words, but in effect opposite to the civil right of the community. . . . These therefore, and the like, who attribute unto the faithful, religious, and orthodox, that is, in plain terms, unto themselves, any particular privilege or power above other mortals, in civil concernments; or *who upon pretext of religion do challenge any manner of authority over such as are not associated with them in their ecclesiastical communion*, I say these have no right to be tolerated by the magistrate; or *neither those that will not own and teach the duty of tolerating all men in matters of mere religion*. For what do all these and the like doctrines signify, but that they may, and are ready upon any occasion to seize the Government, and possess themselves of the estates and fortunes of their fellow subjects; and that they only ask leave to be tolerated by the magistrate so long until they find themselves strong enough to effect it?[20] [Emphasis added.]

Perhaps we must reexamine, then, our assumption that Liberalism always requires absolute governmental neutrality towards religion. If such a respected Liberal theorist as Locke did not believe in strict neutrality, then we as twentieth-century Americans might be justified in questioning this idea as well.

For despite his modern reputation, Locke believed that the government should prohibit not only intolerant religions, but also a few religions that we would consider harmless today:

> Again: That Church can have no right to be tolerated by the magistrate which is constituted upon such a bottom that all those who enter into it do thereby *ipso facto* deliver themselves up to the protection and service of another prince. . . . It is ridiculous for any one to profess himself to be a Mahometan only in his religion, but in everything else a faithful subject to a Christian magistrate, whilst at the same time he acknowledges himself bound to yield blind obedience to the Mufti of Constantinople, who himself is entirely obedient to the Ottoman Emperor, and frames the feigned oracles of that religion according to his pleasure. . . .
>
> Lastly, those are not at all to be tolerated who deny the being of a God. Promises, covenants, and oaths, which are the bonds of human society, can have no hold upon an atheist.[21] [Emphasis in original.]

The government, according to Locke, should not treat atheists, Moslems, and perhaps Catholics ("Mahometans" and "the Mufti of Constantinople" are probably veiled references to Roman Catholics and the Pope) as it does other, "acceptable" religions.

Although I would not go so far as to advocate governmental suppression of atheists, Moslems, or Catholics, I would argue that the government should not treat all religions with strict neutrality.   In official proclamations it might still pretend to be neutral, but in practice it sometimes should take religion into consideration.

Even if publicly admitting to religious considerations might not be wise, the government can still let religion influence its decisions if it does not have to explain them to anyone.   Such discretion Locke would call "prerogative":

Many things there are which the law can by no means provide for, and those must necessarily be left to the discretion of him that has the executive power in his hands to be ordered by him as the public good and advantage shall require.   Nay, it is fit that the laws themselves should in some cases give way to the executive power.   For since many accidents may happen wherein a strict and rigid observation of the laws may do harm . . . it is fit the ruler should have a power in many cases to *mitigate the severity of the law*, and pardon some offenders, since the end of government being the preservation of all, as much as may be, *even the guilty are to be spared where it can prove no prejudice to the innocent*.

This power to act according to discretion for the public good, *without the prescription of the law, and sometimes even against it, is that which is called prerogative*.   For since in some governments the law-making power is not always in being, and is usually too numerous, and so too slow for the dispatch requisite to execution; and because also it is impossible to foresee, and so by laws to provide for all

accidents and necessities that may concern the public,
or make such laws as will do no harm if they are
executed with an inflexible rigour on all occasions
and upon all persons that may come in their way,
therefore there is a latitude left to the executive
power to do many things of choice which the laws do
not prescribe.[22] [Emphasis added.]

Locke thus argues that the executive power should
sometimes use its discretion even to violate the letter of the
law where the spirit of the law or the "public good" would
be better served by not scrupulously following the law. He
also places this prerogative in the hands of the executive,
which is precisely that part of the U.S. government that has
used its discretion by considering religion in the three cases
of this study.

Some would maintain, of course, that such "discretion"
merely justifies governmental dishonesty towards the
public, and that, as Kant might have argued, all
governmental actions and their motivations should be open
for all to see. The government should conceal nothing
behind a wall of "discretion" and should not take actions it
would want to hide from the public. Yet despite its tone of
upstanding righteousness, such an argument ignores the
realities of practical government. First, political
"morality" rarely takes the form of clear-cut, black-and-
white choices. More often, policymakers must distinguish
between a maddening array of moral "gray tones." Without
compromise in the form of an intermediate position between
two extremes, which does not necessarily imply a "moral
compromise," modern politics would become impossible.
Imprisoning a nun convicted of "violating U.S. immigration
law" by feeding and sheltering a family of undocumented
Salvadorans might seem "moral" to the advocates of strict

neutrality. Yet by refusing to take any secret actions that it might have trouble defending in public, the government might thereby punish one of its finest citizens and deliver the Salvadoran family up to possible death by starvation or Central American death squads. More often than not, politics involves choosing among various morally imperfect options rather than selecting the one "moral" choice.

A second objection to the argument for strict neutrality and openness is that, on a purely practical level, the government could not operate if it had to explain all of its actions fully. Even if it wanted to, the government could not be totally open. It performs too many functions and is too large and complex for anyone to explain adequately *what* the government is doing, let alone *why*. As Professor Theodore J. Lowi has noted, past efforts at "open policy openly arrived at," have often proved disastrous.[23]

But I would argue that the government should not want to explain all its actions or even only take actions that it can plausibly explain. The complexities of modern life often defy the best efforts of legislators to regulate them with laws. The executive department must have some leeway to adjust the application of the law to the realities of a particular situation. When they draft a bill, members of Congress cannot possibly foresee all possible situations that might arise, and so the executive department must have some discretion in enforcing the laws that result.

* * * * * *

It seems inevitable that religion and government, church and state, will come into contact, if not mingle, especially since cases such as *Yoder* and since the rise of extensive governmental regulation into almost every area of American society. Yet even if we accept this increased federal presence in our lives, and its accompanying regulation of religion, we may still try to influence how it is to be used. Determining when the government should restrict religion, however, is hardly simple and not without pitfalls. For the dilemma of religious liberty presents two horns: the first would allow all religiously motivated action, including murder, to go unchecked; the second would punish all religiously motivated infractions of the law, no matter how innocuous. The first would permit human sacrifice, while the second would imprison Amish parents for not sending their children to ninth grade. Between these two unacceptable extremes we must find a middle ground.

As indicated above, I would suggest that we question the supposedly Liberal proposition that all religions and religiously inspired actions be treated alike. For if pushed, even most Liberals would probably admit they believe in some definition of acceptable and unacceptable religious belief and action. Few would want to treat a Jim Jones like a Martin Luther King, Jr., even though the "religious beliefs" of both may have inspired them to break the law. One might object that the horrific murders/suicides at Jonestown can scarcely be compared with King's civil disobedience, and I agree; violence, it seems, is where Americans draw the line between acceptable and unacceptable religious or religiously inspired action. Borderline cases, like polygamy among Mormon sects[24] and the use of hallucinogens in Native American rituals,[25] should be tolerated or treated leniently, and indeed often are.[26]

If a religiously inspired act is violent, then, I would maintain it should be prosecuted more severely than other, secularly inspired, crimes, since as a motivation for violence, religion appears stronger and more lasting than secular influences. The bombings and murders by Catholics and Protestants in Northern Ireland and the Shiites in Lebanon, for example, seem more deeply motivated and harder to stop than even the car bombings and contract killings committed by the underworld of New York City. The public, of course, would probably agree and consider a Charles Manson more sinister, and therefore more deserving of harsh treatment, than even an Al Capone. In the public imagination, religious fanaticism as a criminal motivation might seem even more revolting than insanity. I would not, however, advocate harsher treatment for religious groups that are merely new, unusual, or even "spooky," as long as their acts remain nonviolent. Few of today's major religions escaped the epithets "weird," "dangerous," or "cult" at their founding.

If, on the other hand, a religiously motivated act is not violent (e.g., sit-ins, tax evasion, or smuggling), the government should treat the perpetrators more leniently than if the violation were not religiously motivated. In the case of the Sanctuary Movement, for example, it would hardly seem fair to treat religiously motivated alien smugglers who refuse payment for sheltering and feeding aliens in their own homes or churches just as severely as professional alien smugglers who charge exorbitant fees for their "services," and then leave the aliens in the middle of the New Mexican desert to die. The Executive Department should consider a violator's motivation for committing a crime just as a judge does in deciding on the severity of a sentence. As the American jurisprudence of sentencing implies, all violations of the same section of the U.S. code are not alike. It would seem ridiculous to pretend that someone who shot and killed a burglar breaking into his or her home is just as much at fault, and therefore should be punished just as severely, as an underworld operative who beat a rival's child to death with a baseball bat. The motivation of a defendant or potential defendant must influence the government's decision about how to treat such alleged offenders, and religion would seem as good a motivation as any other. Considering religious motivations would not be favoritism because the government should consider *all* of the defendants' motivations, be they religious or not.

To look at my recommendation another way, the treatment should be based on the threat to the civil order; a nonviolent, religiously inspired crime would seem less threatening to the civil order than a comparable secularly inspired crime, but a religiously motivated violent act is more menacing than a comparable secularly inspired act; for as a motivation for lawbreaking, religion exhibits two principal characteristics: 1. it seems to motivate offenders more strongly and longer than secular reasons for breaking the law, and 2. history repeatedly views the acts of "civil disobedience" religion inspires as more ethical than those of the punishing government. One need only consider history's view of the Underground Railroad, the sheltering of Jews during World War II by Dutch Christians, or the "civil disobedience" of Rev. Martin Luther King, Jr. to confirm this second point. To paraphrase Thoreau, those the government labels "criminals" are often the only ones who obey the spirit of the law. To return to my original recommendation, while nonviolent acts, such as sit-ins, tend to attack political parties or the policies of a specific administration, violent ones often attack the entire governmental or societal structure. The government should harshly punish violent religious offenders, then, but practice leniency towards the nonviolent ones; for as Locke wrote, "even the guilty are to be spared where it can prove no prejudice to the innocent."[27] "Criminals" such as Yoder would hardly seem to harm the "innocent."

Table V-2
How Religiously Motivated Offenders Should be Treated (Compared to Secularly Motivated Violators of the Same Statute)

	Leniently	*Same*	*Severely*
Violent			abortion-clinic bombers, Manson
Nonviolent	Yoder, Reynolds, Sanctuary Movement, Hunthausen, Bakker, Moon		

Schematically, then, I would advocate treatment of these real cases following the pattern shown in Table V-2. The way they were treated, however, would look like Table V-3. As these tables show, the government usually seems to use similar criteria when deciding how severely to prosecute religious offenders. These tables also highlight how exceptional the prosecution of Rev. Moon was. Though his "offense" was nonviolent, the government still prosecuted him severely. It is also interesting to note that religion + violence always makes for severe treatment; if anything, the government seems to treat defendants too severely rather than too leniently.

In the above recommendations I would use a definition of religion similar to the one enunciated by the Supreme Court in *Torcaso v. Watkins*. In this case the Court defined "religion" to include "those religions based on a belief in the existence of God" *and* "those religions founded on different beliefs,"[28] including "Buddhism, Taoism, Ethical Culture, Secular Humanism and others."[29] "Religious beliefs," then, would include atheism, "secular humanism," or even a deeply held system of beliefs or values that takes the place of a traditional religion in the life of a defendant. An atheist with deeply held humanitarian beliefs, for example, should not be treated any more severely than a Methodist layperson for sheltering undocumented Central Americans. Indeed, Jim Corbett, the co-founder of the Sanctuary Movement, classifies himself as a Quaker "unbeliever."[30]

Table V-3
How Religiously Motivated Offenders Actually Were Treated (Compared to Secularly Motivated Violators of the Same Statute)

	Leniently	*Same*	*Severely*
Violent			abortion-clinic bombers, Manson
Nonviolent	Yoder, Sanctuary Movement, Hunthausen, Bakker (before 1986)		Moon, Reynolds

If the government is going to take religion into account when deciding how and whether to prosecute, the question arises "Should the government do so openly?" Although to a certain extent the Supreme Court, in cases such as *Yoder*,[31] has already admitted that it considers religion, in my view the government should not explain its consideration of religion much more explicitly. One might perhaps put a statement in the *Principles of Federal Prosecution* or other DOJ guidelines saying that the offender's probable motivation should be considered when deciding whether to prosecute, but nothing more. Prosecutorial decisions, under today's system of "prosecutorial discretion," are secret, and any declarations of blanket exclusions or lenient treatment would inevitably lead to abuse. The government would have to defend openly such positions from attacks by strict libertarians and those not favored with special treatment, a battle it could not win. Drafting, approving, and implementing regulations for religious exceptions to current criminal laws would be an executive agency's nightmare, and such regulations, if it would be possible to implement them, would become too rigid and overly restrict the proper discretionary role of the executive. The government would also put itself in the constitutionally dubious position of defining "religion," and getting a majority of Congress to agree on such a definition would seem well nigh impossible. The government would lose the appearance of neutrality, which could seriously harm its reputation and impede its law enforcement efforts. Given the choice, the government would probably prefer to intimidate a few religiously inspired persons considering breaking the letter of the law, rather than be hoodwinked into excluding from prosecution those who would abuse any open announcement of religious immunity or leniency.

In practice, giving the government any discretion makes it possible for the government to abuse such a "gift." And indeed in Moon's case, the government probably did abuse its discretionary power. Yet, as I have argued above, a government without discretion would be unworkable.

Moon's prosecution for tax fraud also raises the problem of how the government deals with perceived religious threats to its power. In the government's opinion, religious leaders who demand strict obedience from their disciplined followers might sometimes command their disciples to disobey the civil government. The allegiance of the followers would thus be divided, and such a religious leader might threaten the authority of the civil government. Perhaps the public and the government view "cult leaders" in just such a way. They might look upon people like Rev. Moon as immensely powerful figures who at a moment's notice might order their robot-like followers to act against the government. Locke apparently held a similar view of one "cult" of his day: the Roman Catholic Church, disguised in this passage as the Islamic faith:

Again: That Church can have no right to be
tolerated by the magistrate which is constituted upon
such a bottom that all those who enter into it do
thereby *ipso facto* deliver themselves up to the
protection and service of another prince. . . . It is
ridiculous for any one to profess himself to be a
Mahometan only in his religion, but in everything else
a faithful subject to a Christian magistrate, whilst at
the same time he acknowledges himself bound to yield
blind obedience to the Mufti of Constantinople, who
himself is entirely obedient to the Ottoman Emperor,
and frames the feigned oracles of that religion
according to his pleasure.[32]

Locke seems to have viewed the Catholics' allegiance to the
Pope in his day as modern-day Americans view
Unificationists' allegiance to Rev. Moon. Even in what I
would regard as its abuse of "prerogative," then, the federal
government seems to have followed the dictates of Lockean
Liberalism.

Besides contributing to the debate on the proper role of
religion in criminal prosecution, my findings might be
applicable to a broad treatment of similar problems, such as
political dissent. Since a comparison of the Sanctuary
Movement's treatment with that of the abortion-clinic
bombers and of Rev. Moon seems to support my hypothesis
about how American society deals with "deviant" religions
and religiously motivated actions, this study might also help
confirm a similar hypothesis about "deviant" political
beliefs and behavior. Nonconformity has always been
expensive.

Notes

1.   John T. Biermans, *The Odyssey of New Religious Movements: Persecution, Struggle, Legitimation; a Case Study of the Unification Church* (Lewiston, NY: The Edwin Mellen Press, 1986), p. 161.

2.   "Declared Sanctuaries (Nationwide)," in United Methodist Church, General Board of Global Ministries, National Program Division, *Sanctuary: A Ministry of Assistance and Solidarity* (New York, NY: 1986).

3.   Gary MacEoin, ed., *Sanctuary: A Resource Guide for Understanding and Participating in the Central American Refugees' Struggle* (San Francisco, CA: Harper & Row, 1985), pp. 117 & 214.

4.   Ibid., p. 22.

5.   Renny Golden and Michael McConnell, *Sanctuary: The New Underground Railroad* (Maryknoll, NY: Orbis Books, 1986), pp. 202-203.

6.   MacEoin, op. cit., and United Methodist Church.

7.   Biermans, p. 172.

8.   *Holy Spirit Association for the Unification of World Christianity v. Tax Commission,* 55 NY 2d 512 (1982).

9.   Ibid., 55 N.Y.2d 512, 519.

10.   Biermans, p. 170.

11.   Jack Sparks, *The Mind Benders* (Nashville, TN: Thomas Nelson, 1979), pp. 132-133.

12. Ibid., p. 125.

13. John Le Moult, "Deprogramming Members of Religious Sects," 46 *Fordham Law Review* 599, in Biermans, p. 74.

14. U.S. District Court for the Eastern Division of Virginia, docket sheet for Don Benny Anderson, Case No. 83-00159-01, Alexandria, VA, 1983.

15. Charles Bosworth Jr. and Girard Steichen, "Recruits in the 'Army of God,'" *Saint Louis* [MO] *Post-Dispatch,* August 12, 1984, in NewsBank microfiche HEA 78:A11 (1984).

16. Charles Bosworth Jr., "'Army of God' Claims Commitment to 'Holy War' on Abortion," *Saint Louis* [MO] *Post-Dispatch,* August 26, 1982, in NewsBank microfiche HEA 69:A5 (1982).

17. U.S. Congress, House of Representatives, Committee on the Judiciary, Subcommittee on Civil and Constitutional Rights, *Abortion Clinic Violence,* Ninety-Ninth Congress, First and Second Sessions, March 6, 12, and April 3, 1985; and December 17, 1986, Serial No. 115 (Washington, D.C.: Government Printing Office, 1987), p. 578.

18. Ibid., pp. 575 & 578.

19. Mark Travis, "Abortion Clinic Bombers Enter Federal Prison," *Saint Petersburg* [FL] *Times,* June 18, 1985, in NewsBank microfiche HEA 59:B1 (1985).

20. John Locke, *A Letter Concerning Toleration,* in Locke, *Treatise Concerning Civil Government and A*

Letter Concerning Toleration (New York, NY: Appleton-Century-Croft, 1965), pp. 183, 210-212.

21. Ibid., p. 212.

22. John Locke, *Treatise of Civil Government,* paragraphs 159-160, in Locke, pp. 108-109.

23. Theodore J. Lowi, lecture of May 7, 1985, at Cornell University, Ithaca, New York.

24. Scott McCortney, "Arizona Town Wedded to Polygamy, But Some Want a Divorce," *Los Angeles Times,* March 2, 1986, p. 2; however, see *Reynolds v. United States,* 98 U.S. 145 (1878).

25. Stephen Beyer, "Brave New World Revisited: Fifteen Years of Chemical Sacraments," *Wisconsin Law Review,* pp. 879-940 (1980). See, for example, *Native American Church of New York v. United States,* 468 F. Supp. 1247 (S.D.N.Y. 1979).

26. McCartney, p. 2, and *State v. Soto,* 21 Or. App. 794, 537 P.2d 142 (1975); and *State v. Whittingham,* 19 Ariz. App. 27, 504 P.2d 950 (Ct. App. 1973), *cert. denied,* 417 U.S. 946 (1974); see also 21 C.F.R. § 1307.31.

27. Locke, p. 109.

28. *Torcaso v. Watkins,* 367 U.S. 488, 495 (1960).

29. 367 U.S. 495, footnote 11.

30. MacEoin, pp. 187 & 214.

31. *Wisconsin v. Yoder,* 406 U.S. 205 (1972).

32.   Locke, p. 212.

Appendices

Appendix A

Sentencing of Sanctuary Workers

Defendant:[1]	*Counts under which Convicted:*	*Sentence:*
Anthony Clark	1) 8 U.S.C. § 1324(a)(3)	3 years probation

Phillip M. Conger	1) 18 U.S.C. § 371
	2) 18 U.S.C. § 2 &
	     8 U.S.C. § 1324(a)(2)
	3) 18 U.S.C. § 2 &
	     8 U.S.C. § 1325
		5 years probation
		5 years concurrent
		probation
		5 years concurrent
		probation

James A. Corbett	found not guilty of violating 18 U.S.C. § 371	
Cecilia del Carmen Juarez de Emery	1) 8 U.S.C. § 1325 & 18 U.S.C. § 2	2 years probation and 200 hours community service
Maria del Socorro Pardo de Aguilar	1) 18 U.S.C. § 371 2) 8 U.S.C. § 1324(a)(1)	5 years probation 5 years concurrent probation
John B. Elder[2]	1) 18 U.S.C. § 371 2) 18 U.S.C. § 371 3) 8 U.S.C. § 1324(a)(1) 4) 8 U.S.C. § 1324(a)(1) 5) 8 U.S.C. § 1324(a)(2) 6) 8 U.S.C. § 1324(a)(2)	150 days in a halfway house for all counts
Mary Kay Espinosa	found not guilty of violating 8 U.S.C. § 1324(a)(3), 18 U.S.C. § 2, and 8 U.S.C. § 1325	

John M. Fife	1) 18 U.S.C. § 371
	2) 8 U.S.C. § 1324(a)(2)
	     & 18 U.S.C. § 2
	3) 8 U.S.C. § 1324(a)(2)
	     & 18 U.S.C. § 2
		5 years probation
		5 years concurrent
		probation
		5 years concurrent
		probation

Defendant:	*Counts under which Convicted:*	*Sentence:*
Katherine M. Flaherty	1) 8 U.S.C. § 1302, 8 U.S.C. § 1306, & 18 U.S.C. § 2	2 years probation
Margaret Jean Hutchinson	1) 18 U.S.C. § 371	5 years probation
Wendy LeWin	1) 8 U.S.C. § 1324(a)(2)	3 years probation
Nena MacDonald	found not guilty of violating 18 U.S.C. § 371	
Bertha Martel-Benavidez	1) 8 U.S.C. § 1325 & 18 U.S.C. § 2	2 years probation
Stacey Lynn Merkt[3]	1) 18 U.S.C. § 371	179 days in prison
Darlene Nicgorski	1) 18 U.S.C. § 371 2) 8 U.S.C. § 1324(a)(2) & 18 U.S.C. § 2 3) 8 U.S.C. § 1324(a)(3)	5 years probation 5 years concurrent probation 5 years concurrent probation
Anna K. Priester	all counts dismissed	
Ramon Dagoberto Quinoñes	1) 18 U.S.C. § 371 2) 8 U.S.C. § 1325 & 18 U.S.C. § 2	5 years probation 5 years concurrent probation
Mary Waddell	all counts dismissed	

Sources

1.   Unless otherwise indicated, data are from U.S. District Court, Phoenix, AZ, "Active Criminal Docket," *U.S. v. Aguilar, et al.,* CR-85-00008, September 27, 1985.

2.   Ignatius Bau, *This Ground is Holy: Church Sanctuary and Central American Refugees* (Mahwah, NJ: Paulist Press, 1985), pp. 82-83; and *U.S. v. Merkt,* 794 F.2d 950, 953 (1986)

3.   Bau, pp. 82-83.

Appendix B

Sentencing of Abortion-Clinic Bombers

Defendant:[1]	Counts under which Convicted:	Sentence:
Don Benny Anderson[2]	1) 18 U.S.C. § 1952	5 years prison
	2) 18 U.S.C. § 844(i)	5 years consecutive prison
	3) 18 U.S.C. § 371	2 years consecutive prison
Curtis Anton Beseda[3]	1) 18 U.S.C. § 844(i)	10 years prison
	2) 18 U.S.C. § 844(i)	10 years consecutive prison
	3) 18 U.S.C. § 844(i)	5 years probation
	4) 18 U.S.C. § 844(i)	5 years concurrent probation, $289,059 restitution
Brent Paul Braud[4]	1) 18 U.S.C. § 371	2 years prison, $50 fine
Michael Donald Bray[5]	1) 18 U.S.C. § 371	5 years prison
	2) 18 U.S.C. § 371	5 years concurrent prison
	3) 18 U.S.C. § 844(i) & 18 U.S.C. § 2	6 years concurrent prison
	4) 18 U.S.C. § 844(i) & 18 U.S.C. § 2	5 years concurrent prison
	5) 18 U.S.C. § 844(i) & 18 U.S.C. § 2	6 years concurrent prison
	6) 18 U.S.C. § 844(i) & 18 U.S.C. § 2	5 years concurrent prison
	7) 18 U.S.C. § 844(i) & 18 U.S.C. § 2	6 years concurrent prison

Defendant:	Counts under which Convicted:	Sentence:
Carl Cenera[6]	1) 18 U.S.C. § 371	3 years prison, $50 fine
Charles Albert [7] Chesire, Jr.	1) 18 U.S.C. § 844(i), 18 U.S.C. § 371, & 18 U.S.C. § 2	5 years prison, $267,902 restitution
Matthew Goldsby[8]	1) 18 U.S.C. § 844(i) & 18 U.S.C. § 371	5 years probation, $353,704 in restitution
	2) 18 U.S.C. § 2, 26 U.S.C. § 5861(f), & 26 U.S.C. § 5871 3) 18 U.S.C. § 844(i) & 18 U.S.C. § 371 4) 26 U.S.C. § 5861(f) & 26 U.S.C. § 5871 5) 18 U.S.C. § 844(i) & 18 U.S.C. § 371 6) 26 U.S.C. § 5861(f) & 26 U.S.C. § 5871 7) 18 U.S.C. § 844(i) & 18 U.S.C. § 371	10 years prison, plus 5 years probation to be served after leaving prison (for counts 2-7)
David Holman[9]	1) 18 U.S.C. § 844(i)	18 months prison, $50 fine
	2) 18 U.S.C. § 844(i)	3 years probation, $50 fine
Derrick James Jarreau[10]	1) 18 U.S.C. § 371	2 years prison, $50 fine
William H. Lanning[11]	1) 26 U.S.C. § 5861(d) & 26 U.S.C. § 5871	2 years prison
Dennis John Malvasi[12]	1) 18 U.S.C. § 844(i)	6 years prison, $50 fine
	2) 18 U.S.C. § 844(i)	6 years concurrent prison, $50 fine
	3) 18 U.S.C. § 844(i)	1 year consecutive prison
Kenneth William Shields[13]	1) 18 U.S.C. § 371	2 years prison, $50 fine

Defendant:	Counts under which Convicted:	Sentence:
James Simmons[14]	1) 18 U.S.C. § 844(i) & 18 U.S.C. § 371	5 years probation, $353,704 in restitution
	2) 18 U.S.C. § 2, 26 U.S.C. § 5861(f), & 26 U.S.C. § 5871	10 years prison, plus 5 years probation to be served after
	3) 18 U.S.C. § 844(i) & 18 U.S.C. § 371	leaving prison (for counts 2-7)
	4) 26 U.S.C. § 5861(f) & 26 U.S.C. § 5871	
	5) 18 U.S.C. § 844(i) & 18 U.S.C. § 371	
	6) 26 U.S.C. § 5861(f) & 26 U.S.C. § 5871	
	7) 18 U.S.C. § 844(i) & 18 U.S.C. § 371	
Kathren Simmons[15]	1) 18 U.S.C. § 844(i) & 18 U.S.C. § 371	5 years probation, $2,000 fine
Thomas Eugene Spinks[16]	1) 18 U.S.C. § 371	5 years prison
Kaye Wiggins[17]	1) 18 U.S.C. § 844(i) & 18 U.S.C. § 371	5 years probation, $2,000 fine
Frank Wright, Jr.[18]	1) 18 U.S.C. § 371	6 months prison, 2 years probation, $50 fine

Sources

1.   Defendants' names were obtained from the National Abortion Federation, Washington, D.C.

2.   U.S. District Court for the Eastern District of Virginia, Alexandria, VA, docket sheet for Don Benny Anderson, Case No. 83-00159, 1983.

3.   U.S. District Court, Seattle, WA, docket sheet and "Judgment and Commitment Order" for Curtis Anton Beseda, Case No. CR84-222M(C), 1984.

4.   Clerk of the Court, U.S. District Court, Baton Rouge, LA, interview by telephone with author, November 3, 1987.

5.   Clerk of the Court, U.S. District Court, Baltimore, MD, interview by telephone with author, November 10, 1987.

6.   Clerk of the Court, U.S. District Court, Scranton, PA, interview by telephone with author, February 3, 1988.

7.   U.S. District Court, Baton Rouge, LA.

8.   Clerk of the Court, U.S. District Court, Pensacola, FL, interview by telephone with author, October 30, 1987.

9.   U.S. District Court, Northern District of Illinois, Western Division, Rockford, IL, indictment and "Judgment and Probation/Commitment Order" for David Holman, Case No. 87-CR-20001, February and July, 1987.

10.   U.S. District Court, Baton Rouge, LA.

11.   Clerk of the Court, U.S. District Court, Granite City, IL, interview by telephone with author, November 12, 1987.

12.   U.S. District Court for the Southern District of New York, docket sheet and "Judgment and Probation/Commitment Order" for Dennis John Malvasi, Case No. CR-00176-01 (TPG), September, 1987.

13.   U.S. District Court, Baltimore, MD.

14.   U.S. District Court, Pensacola, FL.

15.   Ibid.

16.   U.S. District Court, Baltimore, MD.

17.   U.S. District Court, Pensacola, FL.

18.   U.S. District Court, Scranton, PA.

Selected Bibliography

ABC News, Polling Unit. *ABC News/Washington Post Poll.* Telephone survey on attitudes on abortion and abortion-clinic bombings. New York, NY, January 20, 1985.

Administrative Office of the United States Courts. *United States District Courts Sentences Imposed Chart: Twelve Month Period Ended June 30, 1984.* Washington, D.C.: Government Printing Office, 1986.

American Civil Liberties Union, National Capital Area, Political Asylum Project. "Evidence of Persons Returned from the U.S. to El Salvador and Subsequently Killed, Imprisoned, or Disappeared." Washington, D.C., 1984.

American Medical Association, House of Delegates. *Violence Against Medical Facilities.* Resolution 82. 38th Interim Meeting. Honolulu, HI, December 2-5, 1984.

Anderson, Allen, and the United States Immigration and Naturalization Service, Central Office Intelligence (COINT). "Strategic Assessment: The Sanctuary Movement." Obtained in response to Freedom of Information request of April 29, 1986, by Dr. Michael D. Roe, 397 Sherburne Ave., St. Paul, MN 55103.

Anderson, David E. "Moon Case Called Threat To Religious Freedom." *New Jersey Law Journal*, 112 (1983), p. 621.

Arizona Republic/Phoenix Gazette, Arizona Poll. Survey of attitudes towards the Sanctuary Movement. Phoenix, AZ, January 1985.

Bau, Ignatius. *This Ground is Holy: Church Sanctuary and Central American Refugees.* Mahwah, NJ: Paulist Press, 1985.

Beseda, Curt. "It's Not Terrorism to Stop the Slaughter." *USA Today*, November 23, 1984.

Biermans, John T. *The Odyssey of New Religious Movements: Persecution, Struggle, Legitimation; A Case Study of the Unification Church.* Lewiston, NY: The Edwin Mellen Press, 1986.

Blockson, Charles L. "Escape from Slavery: The Underground Railroad." *National Geographic*, vol. 166, no. 1, July 1984, p. 3.

Bosworth, Charles, Jr. and Girard C. Steichen. "Recruits in the 'Army of God.'" *St. Louis* [MO] *Post-Dispatch*, August 12, 1984. In NewsBank microfiche, HEA 78:A11 (1984).

Boyd, Gerald M. "Reagan Condemns Arson of Clinics." *New York Times*, January 4, 1985, p. A1.

Brown, Rusty. "Sister Darlene Nicgorski." *Ms.*, vol. 45, January 1987, p. 54.

Bureau of National Affairs. *Immigration Reform: A Practical Guide.* Washington, D.C., 1987.

Caplan, Lincoln. *The Tenth Justice.* New York, NY: Alfred A. Knopf, 1987.

CBS News, Election and Survey Unit. "Abortion, 12 Years Later." *CBS News/New York Times Poll.* New York, NY, January 22, 1985.

Cobb, Paul. "Moon Victim of Gov't Conspiracy, Senate Committee Review Exposes Facts." *Oakland Post,* July 3, 1985.

Collins, Sheila D. "The New Underground Railroad." *Monthly Review,* vol. 38, no. 1, May 1986, p. 1.

Colson, Charles. "The Fear of Doing Nothing." *Christianity Today,* vol. 31, May 15, 1987, p. 72.

Commissioner of Internal Revenue and the Chief Counsel for the Internal Revenue Service, U.S. Internal Revenue Service. *Annual Report 1981.* Washington, D.C.: Government Printing Office, 1982.

Corbett, Jim. *The Sanctuary Church.* Pendle Hill Pamphlet 270. Wallingford, PA: Pendle Hill Publications, 1986.

Day, James M., and William S. Laufer, eds. *Crime, Values, and Religion.* Norwood, NJ: Ablex Publishing Corp., 1987.

Donovan, Patricia. "The Holy War." *Family Planning Perspectives,* vol. 17, no. 1, January/February 1985, p. 5.

Eidsmoe, John. *The Christian Legal Advisor.* Milford, Michigan: Mott Media, 1984.

Engel, Margaret, and Lyle V. Harris. "Blast Spurs New Protests: Barry, Falwell Clash Over Clinic Violence." *The Washington Post,* January 2, 1985, p. A1.

Ezell, Harold. "A Call from the Wall." *Voice* (a publication of the Full Gospel Business Men's

Fellowship, International, P.O. Box 50550, Costa Mesa, CA 92628), vol. 34, no. 9, September 1986.

Forrest, Jacqueline Parroch, and Stanley K. Henshaw. "The Harassment of U.S. Abortion Providers." *Family Planning Perspectives,* vol. 19, January/February 1987, p. 9.

Frame, Randy. "Violence Against Abortion Clinics Escalates Despite the Opposition of Prolife Leaders." *Christianity Today,* vol. 29, February 1, 1985, p. 44.

Freedman, Samuel G. "Portrait of an Extremist: Suspect in N.Y. Abortion-Clinic Bombings." *Los Angeles Daily Journal,* vol. 100, May 21, 1987, p 22.

Gallup, George, Jr., et al. "Cults Lead List of Groups 'Not Wanted as Neighbors.'" *The Gallup Report,* January/February 1987, nos. 256-257, p. 19.

Golden, Renny, and Michael McConnell. *Sanctuary: The New Underground Railroad.* Maryknoll, NY: Orbis Books, 1986.

Hager, Jeff. "3 indicted for fires at clinics." [Wilmington, DE] *Evening Journal,* February 13, 1985. In NewsBank microfiche HEA 11:B6 (1985).

Haley, Jim. "Abortion-Clinic Arsonist Given 20 Years." *The* [Everett, WA] *Herald,* December 20, 1984, 3rd edition, p. 1A.

_____. "Terrorist? Martyr? No, Says Arsonist." *The* [Everett, WA] *Herald,* December 19, 1984, 2nd edition, p. 1A.

Harris, Louis. "Americans Abhor Attacks on Abortion Clinics." *The Harris Survey,* #10 (1985).

Hern, Warren M. "With Reagan's Blessing, It's Open Season on Abortion Clinics." *The Los Angeles Daily Journal,* vol. 97, December 31, 1984, p. 4.

Hollander, Cohen Associates. Telephone poll #5000. Baltimore, MD, September 1984.

Irey, Elmer L., and William Slocum. *The Tax Dodgers: The Inside Story of the T-Men's War with America's Political and Underworld Hoodlums.* New York, NY: Greenberg Publisher, 1948.

Jayne, Roxanne E., Joan L. Rosenthal, and Sonia S. Sloan. "Uncivil Disobedience." *Delaware Lawyer,* Fall 1985, p. 10.

Kort, Michele. "Domestic Terrorism: On the Front Line At An Abortion Clinic." *Ms.,* May 1987, p. 48.

"Little or No Change in Attitudes on Abortion; Clinic Bombings Are Universally Condemned." *Family Planning Perspectives,* vol. 17, no. 2, March/April 1985, p. 76.

Locke, John. *Treatise of Civil Government and A Letter Concerning Toleration.* New York, NY: Appleton-Century-Crofts, 1965.

Loder, Ted. *No One But Us: Personal Reflections On Public Sanctuary.* San Diego, CA: LuraMedia, 1986.

Lubasch, Arnold H. "Rev. Moon Goes On Trial in City On Tax Charges." *New York Times,* April 2, 1982, p. B3.

MacEoin, Gary, ed. *Sanctuary: A Resource Guide for Understanding and Participating in the Central American Refugees' Struggle.* San Francisco, CA: Harper & Row, 1985.

Magnuson, Ed. "Explosions Over Abortion: More Clinic Bombings Spur Widespread Concern and Controversy." *Time,* vol. 125, January 14, 1985, p. 16.

May, Lee. "47 in Congress Write to Judge, Ask Leniency in Sanctuary Case." *Los Angeles Times,* July 1, 1986, part I, p. 14.

Merit Report, The. July 29, 1982. New York, NY: Philip Morris, Inc., 1982.

Moley, Raymond. *Politics And Criminal Prosecution.* New York: Minton, Balch & Co., 1929.

"More Ads, No More Bombs." *America,* editorial, vol. 154, February 8, 1986, p. 82.

National Abortion Federation. "Antiabortion Violence: Incidents of Arsons, Bombings, and Attempts, 1977-1987." Statistical report. Washington, D.C., January 1988.

_____. "Incidents of Reported Violence Toward Abortion Providers." Statistical report. Washington, D.C., October 1987.

Pionin, Eric. "Falwell Urges End to Bombings." *The Washington Post,* January 5, 1985, p. A8.

Pruet, George W., Jr., and Henry R. Glick. "Social Environment, Public Opinion, and Judicial Policymaking: A Search for Judicial Representation." *American Politics Quarterly,* vol. 14, nos. 1-2, January-April 1986, p. 5.

Purdum, Todd S. "A Day After Cardinal's Appeal, Bombing Suspect Surrenders." *New York Times,* February 25, 1987, p. B1.

SELECTED BIBLIOGRAPHY   131

Ramsay, Clay. "More on the Sanctuary Movement." *Monthly Review,* vol. 38, no. 4, September 1986, p. 39.

Richardson, Herbert, ed. *Constitutional Issues in the Case of Reverend Moon: Amicus Briefs Presented to the United States Supreme Court.* Lewiston, NY: Edwin Mellen Press, 1984.

Rubin, Alissa. "Bulldog Prosecutor Returns to Paul, Weiss." *The American Lawyer,* November, 1982, p. 101.

Rushing, Ernest L. "The Expanded Jurisprudence of The Religion Clauses: Will The Sanctuary Movement Benefit?" *Gonzaga Law Review,* vol. 21 (1985/86), pp. 177-197.

Scheidler, Joseph M. *Closed: 99 Ways to Stop Abortion.* Westchester, IL: Crossway Books, 1985.

Schneider, Susan. "The War on Sex: Abortion-Clinic Bombing." *Mademoiselle,* April 1986, p. 172.

Sciarrino, Alfred J. "*United States v. Sun Myung Moon*: Precedent for Tax Fraud Prosecutions of Local Pastors?" *Southern Illinois University Law Journal,* 1984, no. 2, p. 237.

Silk, James. *Despite a Generous Spirit: Denying Asylum in the United States.* Washington, D.C.: U.S. Committee for Refugees, American Council for Nationalities Service, 1986.

Sparks, Jack. *The Mindbenders.* Nashville, TN: Thomas Nelson, 1979.

Stewart, James B. *The Prosecutors.* New York, NY: Simon and Schuster, 1987.

Taylor, Steve. "I Blew Up the Clinic Real Good." *I Predict 1990*. Audiotape. Chatsworth, CA: Sparrow Records, 1987.

Tell, Larry. "The Rev. Moon's Money." *The National Law Journal*, May 17, 1982, p. 6.

Thomas, Cal. "Bombing Abortion Clinics: It's Violent, But Why Not?" *Los Angeles Times*, November 27, 1984, part II, p. 5.

Tolan, Sandy, and Carol Ann Bassett. "Operation Sojourner: Informers in the Sanctuary Movement." *The Nation*, vol. 241, July 20/27, 1985, p. 40.

Tomasi, Lydio F., ed. *In Defense of the Alien*. Proceedings of the 1986 Annual National Legal Conference on Immigration and Refugee Policy. New York, NY: Center for Migration Studies, Inc., 1987.

Transcript of Proceedings: Information Meeting on the Cult Phenomenon in the United States. February 5, 1979. Washington, D.C.: Ace Federal Reporters, Inc., 1979.

Tribe, Laurence. "Brief for Appellant Sun Myung Moon." *United States v. Moon*, Case No. 82-1275, U.S. Court of Appeals for the Second Circuit, November 30, 1982.

United Methodist Church, General Board of Global Ministries, National Program Division. *Sanctuary: A Ministry of Assistance and Solidarity*. New York, NY, 1986.

United States Bureau of Alcohol, Tobacco and Firearms. *ATF: Explosives Law and Regulations*. Washington, D.C.: Government Printing Office, 1982.

_____. *Explosive Incidents Report 1986*. Washington, D.C., 1987.

United States Congress, House of Representatives, Committee on the Judiciary, Subcommittee on Civil and Constitutional Rights. *Abortion Clinic Violence.* Ninety-Ninth Congress, First and Second Sessions, March 6, 12, and April 3, 1985; and December 17, 1986, Serial No. 115. Washington, D.C.: Government Printing Office, 1987.

_____. Senate, Committee on the Judiciary, Subcommittee on the Constitution. *Issues in Religious Liberty.* Ninety-Eighth Congress, Second Session, June 26, 1984, Serial No. J-98-124. Washington, D.C.: Government Printing Office, 1984.

United States Department of Justice. *Principles of Federal Prosecution.* Washington, D.C.: Government Printing Office, 1980.

United States District Court for the Southern District of New York. "Judgment and Probation/Commitment Order for Dennis John Malvasi." Docket No. S87 Cr.00176-01 (TPG). New York, NY, 1987.

United States Immigration and Naturalization Service. "Asylum Cases Filed with District Directors: Fiscal Year 1987 through September 1987." Computer printout. Washington, D.C., 1987.

Werner, Leslie Maitland. "Abortion Bombings Give Once-Anonymous Agency New Notoriety." *Los Angeles Daily Journal,* vol. 99, February 4, 1985, p. 3.

Selected Legal Citations

Berman v. United States, 156 F.2d, 377 (9th Cir.), *cert. denied*, 329 U.S. 795 (1946).

Bob Jones University v. United States, 103 S. Ct. 2017 (1983).

Everson v. Board of Education, 330 U.S. 1 (1947).

Holy Spirit Association for the Unification of World Christianity v. Tax Commission, 55 N.Y.2d 512 (1982).

Reynolds v. Unites States, 98 U.S. 145 (1878).

Roe v. Wade, 410 U.S. 113 (1973).

State v. Soto, 21 Or. App. 794, 537 P.2d 142 (1975).

State v. Whittingham, 19 Ariz. App. 27, 504 P.2d 950 (Ct. App. 1973), *cert. denied*, 417 U.S. 946 (1974).

Torcaso v. Watkins, 367 U.S. 488 (1960).

United States v. Aguilar, et al., U.S. District Court, Phoenix, AZ, Case No. CR-85-00008-01 through -16, filed January 10, 1985.

United States v. Elder, 601 F. Supp. 1574 (1985).

United States v. Merkt, 764 F.2d 266 (5th Cir. 1985).

United States v. Merkt [and Elder], 794 F.2d 950 (5th Cir. 1986), *cert. denied*, 107 S. Ct. 1603 (1987).

United States v. Moon, 532 F. Supp. 1360 (1982), 718 F.2d 1210 (1983), *cert. denied*, 466 U.S. 971 (1984).

United States v. Seeger, 380 U.S. 163 (1965).

Wisconsin v. Yoder, 406 U.S. 205 (1972).

Index

STUDIES IN AMERICAN RELIGION